Stanley K. Sheinbaum
A 20th Century Knight's Quest for Peace, Civil Liberties and Economic Justice
(A Memoir)
Stanley K. Sheinbaum with William A. Meis, Jr.

ISBN: 0615570224
ISBN-13: 9780615570228

Credits:
Poem quoted in the Prologue: "Ozymandias," by Percy Bysshe Shelley, 1818.

All song credits for the lyrics which begin chapters are provided, except for those in the epilogue which are, in order of their appearance: "Sing, Sing, Sing," lyrics by Louis Prima, music by Ziggy Elman, 1936. "I Can't Get Started," lyrics by Ira Gershwin music by Vernon Duke, 1936. "It Might As Well Be Spring," lyrics by Oscar Hammerstein II, music by Richard Rodgers, 1945. "T'ain't What You Do It's the Way That You Do It," lyrics by Melvin "Sy" Oliver, music by James "Trummy" Young, 1937. "Thanks For The Memories," lyrics by Leo Robin, music by Ralph Rainger, 1938. "Where Or When," lyrics by Lorenz Hart, music by Richard Rodgers 1937. "Moonglow" lyrics by Edie DeLange, music by Will Hudson and Irving Mills.

All photos are from Sheinbaum family albums or by unknown photographers except those where known credits are given.

Cover and book design by William A. Meis, Jr.

Chapter heading graphic designs are original doodles created by Stanley Sheinbaum.

For Betty, without whom
I might never have found
my way, and for all
my friends who kept me
on the path

CONTENTS

ACKNOWLEDGMENTS

A biographical memoir of a long, long life evolves from the collective consciousness of many people, but special mention must be made of previous lengthy interviews conducted by Joan Didion, Robert Scheer, Ron Brownstein, Alan Jolis, and especially Dale E. Treleven and William Benschoten under the auspices of the Oral History Program, University of California, Los Angeles. Moreover, documents from Stanley's legendary career in economics and international relations reside in the Stanley K. Sheinbaum collection at the University of California, Santa Barbara, archived under the direction of David Tambo UCSB, Head of Special Collections. Much of the material at UCSB was originally organized and archived by the wonderfully efficient Jean Anderson without whom much would have been lost. And of course the anecdotes, stories, analysis, and memories of Betty Warner Sheinbaum are threaded throughout.

Numerous individuals read all or parts of the material and contributed suggestions that have improved the content and the style of the work. Matthew Sperling, Elizabeth Bauer, Richard Parker, Steve Wasserman, Al Rubin, Gil Sheinbaum, Morgan Meis, Stefany Golberg, and Timothy Don were particularly helpful. Narda Zacchino's generous gift of time and attention provided an essential final editorial review and polish.

Stanley's hard-working and devoted staff were essential to providing support and information. Marti Maniates has worked with Stanley and Betty for more than 27 years, and is an especially valuable resource for the many details concerning their lives and Stanley's career. Robert (Bob) Stoneman has been with the Sheinbaums' for over 37 years (he started working for them when he was 8 years old). Stephanie Harker coordinates the many political and philanthropic salons and events at their home. Aj Trotter assisted with the numerous edits, error corrections and omissions of the manuscript. She also catalogued and prepared the wonderful photographs. Furthermore, this book would not have been possible without the assistance of Stanley's personal caregivers, Paul Pedraza, Nereo Cruz, and Luz Martinez who has cared for various members of the family for over 18 years.

Finally, many thanks to Nathan and Lillian Gardels who brought Meis and Sheinbaum back together from the early days of NPQ to collaborate on writing this memoir. And to Sabine Huemer, whose counsel, support, and love allowed co-author Meis to focus on the life of Stanley K. Sheinbaum.

PROLOGUE:
Stardust

Sometimes I wonder why I spend, the lonely night dreaming of a song. "Stardust," lyrics by Mitchell Parish, music by Hoagy Carmichael, 1929.

Hi. I'm Stanley Sheinbaum, Stanley K. Sheinbaum, and I'm fading. Don't be too concerned. I plan to be around for a while longer, but after a long life during which I ate with and argued with, fought with and defended presidents and prime ministers, princesses and kings, movie stars, parliamentarians, priests, rabbis, imams, convicts and criminals, people with money beyond even your wildest dreams, and innumerable members of Congress, honest and dishonest, even a writer or two, all of it while just trying to create a little peace and justice in this unjust world, I now spend more and more time resting and reflecting on all those things I've done, the places I've been, and the people I've known…the memories, all the memories…*Thanks for the memories*…But who am I thanking? After all, they're *my* memories. So I take this time to thank myself, fade into myself, enjoy and appreciate myself and let life go on around me as those who love and care about me wish my daily life to be…

But me? Well my important life, my inside life, is spent trying to reconstruct what my time on earth has meant, not to my friends and family, not even to my loved ones, but to me. What did all this scurrying about all over the city, the state, the country, the world come to? Did I really accomplish anything positive, or am I like that statue in the desert, that …*colossal wreck, boundless and bare,* out from which *the lone and level sands stretch far away.* I'm sure that's from a poem, too lyrical for me to have said it. But I don't remember the name of the poem. I must have read it in high school, or maybe college, probably college since I didn't take high school very seriously. To be honest, I don't remember why I remember those particular words, but that fragment has always stayed locked away in my brain. Why that particular fragment? You tell me, after you've read my story, after you've thought about my life.

Okay, so I sleep a great deal, and my sleeping upsets a lot of people around me, but it doesn't upset me and I want to tell you why: because when I sleep, I am most like I once was—aware, passionate and engaged. I will presume that doesn't make sense to you so let me share a little secret of my old age: as my body declines and I become less interested in the conscious world around me, my dreams become more vivid and real. I remember facts, events, everyday occurrences, and if I'm riding on a good dream, almost everything! I converse and argue with all the characters in my life. I sing my favorite songs from long ago. I actually do have answers to all the intractable problems I worked to solve when I was young. I bring peace to the Middle East; I design an economy that continues to create wealth without enormous income disparities between rich and poor; I end war as a weapon of foreign policy; I even make love to Jean Harlow…more than once, mind you. My dream life is a wonderful life, so, I prefer to live in my dreams most of the time. Wouldn't you?

But I do want you to know about my life, so I found someone to listen to my stories and put them down on paper so you can read them at your leisure. Why would you bother? Well, first of all, as the guy who's listening to me says, "It's a hell of a good story!" He's laughing now because I'm telling you that, but it *is* a hell of a good story. After a rather rough start and some early dilly-dallying around, I managed to become a major player in many of the momentous public events that happened during my ninety plus years. And right now, during this time when America appears mired in stagnation, anger and hopeless frustration, I truly believe that reading about me, a reasonably intelligent but not brilliant Jewish kid who grew up in New York City during the Great Depression, failed in school, spent the war years in a map-making unit stateside, returned to high school as a 26-year-old and started at a college on the GI Bill in a cow town in Oklahoma, still somehow managed to become an advisor to those presidents, kings, princesses and prime ministers. This shows what can happen if one simply pushes through and believes in certain basic principles of how things should be and then sticks to those principles through good times and bad. Being positive, I guess. I'm saying that in some mysterious way, the American Dream still works, and my life is a pretty good example of the American Dream. We need to believe in that dream. We need to believe we can accomplish great things.

Okay, if you know anything at all about me before you started reading this, you might find it odd that I'm arguing in favor of the American Dream since I'm so fond of saying that America is failing and that our country is in deep, deep trouble. Well, I'm not really fond of saying that; not at all. I don't want my country to fail, but I do believe we are in serious danger because we've stopped believing we can be better and do better. We have replaced a dream that we can accomplish great things with a dream that we can escape into a past that never was. Believe me, I've lived a long, long time, and the past wasn't so damn hot. It really wasn't. What was great, what made things seem so much better was that we believed tomorrow would be better than today. Nowadays, we believe tomorrow will probably be worse. That's no good.

Look, I know for certain that in one way of looking at things, *my* tomorrow *will* be worse. After all, I don't have that much time left. But in my dream state, in my ideal state, in my memories and my songs and my fugue ramblings, I still care, I'm still involved, I still believe tomorrow will be better. And that's why I remain so optimistic. If I've learned anything over the years, I've learned it's not so important whether we win the battles what really matters is that we continue to fight the battles—for justice, for equality, for fairness, so that we can *crown thy good with brotherhood from sea to shining sea*. That's America isn't it? "America The Beautiful" as we like to sing. My America.

So, as you read this story, think of it as your story, or better yet, our story. After all, I'm just a man, like every other man and woman in this country. Think of my struggles as our struggles, how we can find happiness and fulfillment in fighting more than in winning, how the greatest joy comes from those moments of anticipation before the encounter—that feeling of rapture that comes over us when we realize we're going to pull ourselves together and try one more time to make the world a better place. That's all that matters. Really. Trust me. I know. I've been there.

CHAPTER ONE
How Deep Is the Ocean?

How can I tell you what is in my heart? …How deep is the ocean? How high is the sky? "How Deep Is The Ocean," lyrics and music Irving Berlin, 1931

I didn't like Selma Klimberg very much. Although she was born in the United States and raised in New York City, she was very *Galitzian*— Jewish from the old Austrio-Hungarian Empire's Polish province of Galicia. *Galitzianer* saw themselves as superior to Jews from other parts of Eastern Europe, and Selma Klimberg definitely thought she was superior. She even looked down on her own brothers because they were, in her mind at least, involved with the "entertainment business." In fact, they did run a well-known San Francisco establishment called the Koffee Kup on the restaurant side and the Rumpus Room on the cabaret side. I'm sure it was the Rumpus Room that bothered her most.

Although pictures show she could be an attractive woman, I don't remember Selma as beautiful or pretty. I don't remember her as being particularly kind to anyone. Certainly not to me. Actually, now that I think back on it, I didn't really like Selma Klimberg at all. But I guess I should have; she was my mother.

When I was a young boy, we lived in a spacious new apartment building on the Upper West Side of New York at 111th and Broadway near Columbia University. My mother was able to afford hired help. Our family was well-respected. Life was good, very good, until one day I came home from school, and my mother was extremely angry, even more upset than usual. "This is going to be your last night in this apartment," she said to me. "Tomorrow we're moving to an awful place called Flatbush. That's in Brooklyn, or so I'm told by your idiot father." I looked at my father, whose handsome face was pale and drawn. "We're broke," my mother added. She turned to my father, "Tell him. Tell him how you really screwed up this time. Tell your son." I looked at my father. He slowly nodded. "I've lost everything, Stanley. There's nothing left." It was 1929, the beginning of the Great Depression.

I hated Flatbush. Even at nine years old, I knew we were not in Flatbush on our way up but on our way down, and I didn't like being poor. Manhattan was rich, beautiful, exciting. Flatbush was poor, ugly and boring. I remember it was the boredom I hated most. It was boring, and I didn't like the kids around me. Most of them were rough, tough, little bastards. So I was a little bit scared and a lot bored. I used to walk by the Lexington Express #4 station on Atlantic Avenue and dream of taking the train back to Morningside Heights and our old life.

Many, many years later, I was at a Hollywood dinner party talking about my days in Flatbush, when my good friend Barbra Streisand leaned across the table. "Stanley," she said, "so why are you running down Flatbush?"

"Hated it," I said.

"Hey, Stanley, I was born in Flatbush." She laughed.

So okay, maybe I am too hard on Flatbush, but I was long gone by the time Barbra was born because our family did move back to Manhattan. Not to luxury, mind you. Not by a long shot! Gilbert Harold, my younger brother arrived while we were still in Flatbush, so five of us, my older brother, Herbert Herman Sheinbaum, the baby, Gilbert, my father, my mother, and I were all living in a single room in the Hotel Regent on the northwest corner of 104th and Broadway. My father was struggling, my mother was forced to sell silk stockings, and I was delivering flowers and selling the *Saturday Evening Post* on the corner of 110th and Broadway. But we were in Manhattan again, so I was happy.

It's funny, you know, but as I look back on those Depression years, I do remember that everyone was really worried, scared even, but my day-to-day life, my child life, was still filled with excitement and adventures. I really was happy most of the time, after we left Flatbush anyway. We were never actually hungry and we had warm clothes and a place to live. For a young kid like me, that was enough to remove any sense of urgency, so I spent most of my time dreaming up schemes to entertain myself.

One of my favorite games was to fool the process servers who hung around the front door of the hotel trying to catch my father. If I saw one I would walk out the front door and ask, "Can I help you, sir?"

"We need to speak to your father, son."

"Oh, he just left a little while ago, but he should be back any minute."

And then while they were hanging around the front door, my father would slip out the back. Sometimes they hung around for a very long time.

I liked my father, partly because, when he was the target of my mother's frustration, she wasn't harping at me. I've never really figured out why my mother made my father's life so difficult because he worked very hard. His name was Herman Sheinbaum, and he made specialty belts for the *shmatte* trade, the garment business. For many years he was very successful running his own company, so my mother had things pretty easy. When times changed and the economy collapsed, that obviously wasn't my father's fault. He didn't cause the hard times, but then, sure, the Depression probably only brought out all the tensions between them that had boiled just below the surface anyway. But I don't know what those deeper tensions were. Truly, I don't, no matter how hard I think about it.

My father was originally from Brest-Litovsk, now just Brest, a city that was, way back in the 14th century, one of the original Jewish settlements in what was then Lithuania and later Belarus, near the Polish border. (It later became famous as the site where the Bolsheviks signed the treaty that withdrew Russian forces from World War I.) Anyway, the family story is that Herman, like so many young Jewish men in the early years of the 20th century, walked across Europe to get on a boat to America. Whether that's true or not, I don't know, but I do know he landed in Boston, and did very well in Salem, Massachusetts. Then he moved to New York where he did even better until 1929.

My father was not only hard-working, he was a resourceful man, a real entrepreneur who liked to take risks. That's probably why the Depression hit his businesses particularly hard. Yet somehow, each time he lost everything, he managed to raise money, probably from loan sharks, to launch a new business. Then he'd buy a dozen sewing machines, hire workers, and turn out women's belts again. He would work his ass off, fourteen, sixteen-hour days, then fall back into bankruptcy under section 77B of the old 1933 Bankruptcy Act because times were so difficult. But he was never deterred by failure. I admired that about him, and I learned from him—learned failure wasn't the end of the world. He would just start up another business and push his way through another cycle, another crisis. Both my older brother Herbert and I worked for him on the sewing machines from time to time. I can still sew a pretty good stitch. Really. Even though I'm an old man now, you put me in front of a machine and I'll show you. It automatically comes back to me. It's in my blood.

So anyway, once we moved back to Manhattan my life immediately picked up. I got back together with my old friends. I remember we used to play stoop ball on the steps in front of the Episcopal Cathedral Church of Saint John the Divine, that sort of creepy, massive gray stone church over on Amsterdam. We gathered around the steps as if we were the Yankees on a baseball diamond, then Irving "Lefty Gomez" would "pitch" a hard rubber ball against the edge of a step at which point the ball would fly up into the air as if it were hit by a batter. Then Lenny "Lou Gehrig," Benny "Babe Ruth" or me, Stanley "Tony Lazzeri" would try to catch the ball on the fly. Whoever caught it would get to be the next pitcher.

Other days we would somehow scrape together enough change to go to the movies. It didn't take much, a nickel or maybe a dime. In those days, the movies were entertainment for poor people. We saw The Marx Brothers in *Monkey Business* and *Horse Feathers*, maybe Johnny Weissmuller in *Tarzan*. Bela Lugosi scared the piss out of me in *Dracula*. We were often a pretty rowdy bunch in the darkened theater, but when Bela Lugosi was on the screen, we were exceedingly quiet and hunched down in our seats.

I also remember warm summer nights when we'd go to John Philip Sousa band concerts at the amphitheater in Central Park. Those concerts were my first real exposure to the patriotic side of American life. I remember there was flag waving and singing and adults would talk about how great it was to be in America even when times were hard. As they listened to the martial music, sometimes I'd overhear their conversations about why life was even harder in other countries, but that didn't mean anything to me since I only knew what life was like in New York. I didn't know Poland from Germany or Austria from Hungary or why Russians were all bad communists.

It was around that time, it must have been in the spring of 1936, when I had my first of those many serendipitous moments that have happened to me throughout my life. I was in a Boy Scout troop that had its meetings at my school on 109th Street, PS 165, which, by the way, I'm told is now one of the best public schools in the city, named PS 165 Robert E. Simon after the developer who once owned Carnegie

Hall. Anyway, back then, I was standing over on Broadway watching the St. Patrick's Day parade dressed in my khaki scout uniform with my yellow scarf and khaki cap when a big black Cadillac convertible stopped right in front of me. A jovial man in a bowler hat and bow tie was sitting in the back seat and waving toward the crowds when he motioned for me to approach his car. As I came near, the man smiled and said to me: "Hop in, son, and join the parade!"

I hesitated for a moment. I knew I wasn't supposed to get into cars with strangers, but I didn't think this man in this parade was the sort of incident my mother had warned me about, so I jumped into the car. As we headed down Broadway toward Times Square, I realized I was riding with Al Smith, 1928 Democratic presidential nominee against Herbert Hoover, and Alf Landon, the Democratic presidential candidate in '36. Smith was an ex-New York governor, the first Roman Catholic to be nominated for president and also a candidate for the Democratic presidential nomination in the '32 race. He smiled at me and said, "You know, you can wave too, son. People love the Boy Scouts." So I waved. The people waved back. And I loved it. I really loved it.

My parade experience with Smith and Landon was a powerful antidote to the corrosive effects of my mother's constant criticism that I wasn't good enough. It was always: "Stanley, you have to work harder," or "Stanley, don't spend your time goofing around with your stupid friends," or "Stanley, you have to do better in school. Don't end up an idiot like your father." All this despite the fact that for a time, I had actually been an excellent student and been moved ahead two or three grades. So, I rebelled. In fighting against the inevitable feeling that I was no good, I, of course, became no good. Especially in school. I mean, I really screwed up. When I left, at sixteen, from DeWitt Clinton High School in the Bronx, I had the very minimum grade point average you could have and still graduate. Later, I regretted those grades, but at the time, I just didn't care.

For all my mother's *Galitzian* morality, she wasn't religious at all. Nor was my father, but I remember that for some reason I was bar mitzvahed in an Orthodox storefront shul somewhere on the Upper West Side. It must have been to make my grandmother happy. She didn't speak any English so we communicated in our own special sign language. I remember her big smile on her wrinkled, round little face when she hugged me outside the shul after the ceremony was over. Well, I was officially a man! Except I really wasn't much of a man at all. Or at least I wasn't a very responsible one in those days.

For example, in yet another attempt to get on my mother's good side, I used to tell her I was going to the library to study so I could get better grades and become the doctor, the lawyer, even the dentist she wanted me to be. But then, when I reached 125th Street, I turned right toward the Apollo Theater instead of left toward the New York Public Library. Well, maybe it was for the best because I learned more at the Apollo than I would have ever learned at the library.

While it was not uncommon to see whites around the Apollo in those days, it was definitely Harlem and the heart of New York City's black culture. I saw Jimmie Lunceford, Duke Ellington and Chick Webb. This was before swing went mainstream, so white musicians like Tommy Dorsey also played there, and that was where I first heard Benny Goodman.

Later on, during many afternoons when I was supposed to be looking for a job, I hung out at the Paramount Theater in Midtown listening to Benny Goodman's band—you know, he had Gene Krupa on drums, and Teddy Wilson on piano and Lionel Hampton on vibes. The way it worked back then in the movie theaters was that there would be a movie, then a band, then another showing of the movie, then the band would come back. Swing was breaking out. Kids were jitterbugging in the aisles. It was one of those seminal times like rock in the '50s and punk in the '70s. I think one afternoon I must have seen *Maid of Salem* with Claudette Colbert and Fred MacMurray at least five times late into the evening so I could have one more chance to listen to Benny Goodman.

But I first learned to love music at the Apollo, and it was not only the music. There was the dancing. Although I never danced, I saw a sense of relaxed freedom that I had never seen before. Of course times were at least as hard, actually harder I'm sure, in Harlem, but people walked with more of a bounce in their step, they spoke more loosely, they acted unconcerned about how bad things were. For an uptight Jewish kid harassed by his mother, life at the Apollo appeared, on the surface at least, to be another world. And so I learned one more valuable lesson I have carried with me throughout my life: if you act relaxed and confident, people will perceive you are relaxed and confident no matter what you might be feeling inside.

Maybe it was that new attitude that got me into the theater world. Yes, after I left high school I was actually involved in Broadway theater for a while, in a production called *Yokel Boy* at the Majestic on 44th between 7th and 8th in the heart of the theater district. That theater is still there and still a major Broadway venue. Anyway, *Yokel Boy* starred

Buddy Ebsen, Dixie Dunbar, Phil Silvers, and Judy Canova. I got involved because I was hanging out on the street one day and an old high school friend asked me if I wanted to help him work for this play, which turned out to be *Yokel Boy*. I had nothing better to do, and I thought about all the pretty girls, so I said yes. The fourth day I'm there, my friend doesn't show up so the stage manager asks me if I want to be the assistant stage manager.

Okay, well, the problem was that I knew my friend's father was the gangster, Waxey Gordon, who worked with Arnold Rothstein and Meyer Lansky. I didn't want to have my legs broken. Or worse. But it turned out my friend didn't want the job anymore, so I took over as assistant stage manager which was just a fancy name for the guy who did everything no one else wanted to do.

Working on *Yokel Boy* was a lot of fun and I was able to make some very good money on the side. How? Well, one day Phil Silvers stopped me. "Hey kid," he growled, "so, you're allowed to go in and out the stage door there while the play's actually going on aren't ya'?"

"Yes, Mr. Silvers."

"Hey, call me, Phil, kid. By the way, you know that joint across the street, Ralph's Bar and Grill?"

"Yeah, sure, Mister...I mean, Phil."

"Well there's a man sitting in the back booth, name of Frankie. Here's five bucks. Tell him Astroland to win in the sixth."

"Yeah sure, Phil.

I turned to go. "Oh and kid, here's two bits to keep for yourself." He flipped me a quarter.

I thanked him. That was a nice little tip during the Depression. And pretty soon I was running back and forth across the street all night placing bets for a lot of the guys in the cast. Some of the girls as well. It turned out the Frankie, who was making book on the day's races, was Frank Costello, another big gangster. You can be sure I made a hell of a lot more money placing bets for the theater people than I did as the assistant stage manager.

As I guess you can tell, my life was pretty wild with the theater and the showgirls and the gambling, but at the same time I was hanging out with my other friends, upper-middle class types, all of whom went to Columbia and pledged Tau Epsilon Phi, TEP, the Jewish fraternity. I practically lived at the TEP house, although I couldn't be a member since I didn't go to Columbia, didn't go to college at all, had no money to pay for it and, frankly, I was having much too much fun. And all my TEP brothers thought my life was so much more exciting than theirs, but after awhile I became painfully aware that I was becoming a different person than they were.

One afternoon I was sitting in the lounge of the frat house and Lenny and Al were talking about *Sister Carrie*, and I think it was Lenny who made the remark that he wouldn't mind having a Sister Carrie of his own, on the side.

"But why would you want to have a nun for a girlfriend?" I blurted out.

Al said, "He's talking about the Dreiser novel, Stanley. You know, Theodore Dreiser."

I just stared at them.

"Obviously he doesn't," said Lenny. "But why should he? He's gets to hang around showgirls every night."

"Yeah," I said, "that's right, Al." But I was terribly embarrassed and I realized I was really falling behind, losing out, living aimlessly.

I was feeling touchy, already annoyed when I dropped by our apartment where mother was praising my little brother Gilbert's latest report card—all A's, as usual.

"Why don't I ever get any praise?" I said as I glared at my mother.

"There isn't much to praise, Stanley."

"Thanks to you," I threw back at her. Gilbert's little jaw dropped, and he just stared at me. No one talked back to our mother like that.

My mother was enraged. She flew out of her chair and stood before me, trembling. "Get out of here," she screamed, "Get out, and I don't care if you never come back!"

"Why would I want to come back to this dump and a mother like you," I shouted at her.

I felt the sting as she slapped me across the face, and I then whipped around and stormed out the door.

Not long after that incident, I ran into Jay, another old friend who was managing the amusement park at Jones Beach out on Long Island. He told me on a Friday afternoon that he was going to Galveston to open up a version of Jones Beach down there. "Galveston?" I asked, "Never heard of it.".

"Texas," he said.

"Cowboys?"

"I don't think so. It's an island or something, near Houston."

"Houston, Texas."

"Yeah," he said. "Texas, but not the cowboy part. Texas, the land of opportunity right now. Forget the Depression, there's jobs and money everywhere in Texas."

Texas. Stanley Sheinbaum in Texas. Now that sounded different. It sounded like a good place to go to get away, away from my life which was going nowhere.

"When are you leaving?" I asked.

"Monday morning," he said. "You want to come along?"

Well, crazy as it sounds, Monday morning I joined him in his old green 1930 Chevy Sedan and we drove out of New York City across America toward Texas. And so, on that day, the long journey that has become my life began in earnest.

Since then, I still hear my mother's voice pushing me, criticizing me, telling me I need to do more. And it bothers me. But I must also admit, from the perspective of old age, that it is just possible that my mother created my extraordinary life. If 1929 hadn't happened, if we had stayed comfortable, if she hadn't pushed and pushed, pushed me so hard I flew right out the door all the way to Texas, I might have ended up like my older brother who was, frankly, a Willy Loman character with lost dreams, a good, decent salesman, but a very ordinary man. And my life has certainly not been ordinary.

One last story about my mother. A few years after I left New York, when I was drafted into the army during World War II, my First Sergeant at Fort Leonard Wood told me I had to fill in the space for my middle name.

"I don't have a middle name," I said. "There wasn't one on my birth certificate."

"Fill it in anyway," he grumbled with typical army logic.

One doesn't argue with his sergeant, so I decided to use my mother's maiden name, Klimberg. But then I realized I didn't know how to spell it. Was it Klim, Klem, berg, burg? So I just put down the initial "K," and all the rest of my life I've been Stanley K. Sheinbaum. So she's always been part of me. And I guess, when all is said and done, I've wanted it that way.

CHAPTER TWO
This Is The Army, Mr. Jones

We all have been selected from city and from farm. They asked us lots of questions, they jabbed us in the arm... "This Is The Army, Mr. Jones," lyrics and music Irving Berlin, 1942.

So, I met my pal Jay early on that Monday morning. I think he was surprised I actually showed up, but he was in an upbeat mood, eager to get going. He smiled. "Glad you made it. You can do some of the driving."

"Sorry," I said. "I don't know how to drive." He hesitated. "Well," he laughed, "I guess you'll just have learn along the way." I liked that idea.

As we were leaving New York and passing through New Jersey, he turned and asked me, "So what did your mom and dad say about you heading out for Texas?"

"Not much," I offered.

"They didn't try to talk you out of it?"

"Actually, they were glad to see me go. My mother anyway. My father looked like he wanted to come with me."

"Family troubles, huh?"

"No...well, yeah, I guess, but it's not that bad." I thought about my family, but I didn't want to talk badly about them. "My little brother, Gilbert, he said he would miss me."

"Yeah. That's nice...bet you'll miss him too, right?"

"Yeah, sure. I guess."

We drove south down the Atlantic Coast, then across Georgia, Mississippi, Alabama and Louisiana. The roads were less crowded in the South, and sometimes we'd go for miles without seeing another car, so I learned to drive on those roads. It was pretty easy once I managed to shift gears without grinding, although I almost ran off the road when I tried to pass a family traveling in a mule wagon. The mother and father were hunched over on the front bench and the back was filled with dirty, skinny little kids jumping around and playing on the wagon bed. They waved at us and I tried to wave back. That's when I went a little too far onto the left shoulder and came close to scrapping against an old cypress tree with moss hanging from the branches. But I missed it and we were all right.

We arrived in Texas, in Galveston, around three days after we left New York. We were both more than ready to start something new, and Galveston immediately looked less downbeat than many of the places we'd driven past on the road. A lot of the buildings looked fairly new, and there were lots of people on the streets. It felt good.

Our first evening in Galveston, Jay had a business meeting with his investors, the ones who wanted to start an amusement park, so I went for a walk by the waterfront. It was very hot and humid—like August days back in New York, but it was late fall in Galveston so I felt like I'd really arrived in a very different place. And there were palm trees, and pelicans, and I could smell the salty sea air which I never could back home even though New York is near the ocean. Galveston just seemed very exotic to a young man who grew up in a huge metropolis like New York and at that point in my life I had never been anywhere else.

As I was passing the doorway of a neon-lit bar, a young woman in a thin, flower-print dress, curly blond hair, and a lazy sort of smile lifted her hand and more or less waved toward me. "How ya' doin?" she drawled.

I was startled. "Great, fine, thank you." Well, I thought to myself, the girls are very friendly here in Texas.

"Wanna' have a drink?" She said.

"Yeah, sure I…" And then it hit me. Maybe a little too friendly? "Ummm, except I have to be somewhere…" I looked at my watch, "in just fifteen minutes."

"No problem. Good-lookin' guy like you, I can make you happy in fifteen minutes." She pouted. I was young; she was pretty in a shiksa sort of way. I was sorely tempted because she probably could have, but I walked on by.

Later, I found out Jay had neglected to tell me that Galveston in those days was a wild and wooly port town with sailor bars and hookers and brawls at 2:00 a.m. Back in 1900, Galveston was devastated by a monster Category 4 hurricane which killed more than 8,000 people, so the remaining citizens decided the quickest route to recovery was to turn their little island off the Texas coast into the Sin City of the Gulf. So I had fun staying there for a few weeks, but I quickly realized Galveston was hardly the place to start my new life, go to college, and get established. I'm not even sure they had a college in Galveston in 1939.

Because I wanted more than Galveston had to offer, one morning I said farewell to Jay, went downtown to the bus station, and took a Greyhound inland to Houston—about fifty miles away by highway but a whole different planet away when it came to opportunities for school and work. The very next day, when I was pounding the pavement in the industrial section of east central Houston, I saw a faded blue sign with white lettering indicating the business was a photo-lithography printer: Rein Company Printers. One of my many jobs in New York had been in a printing plant, so I took a chance, walked into Rein's, and asked if they needed help. The receptionist told me she didn't think so, but I could sit there in the reception area and wait if I wanted to talk with the plant manager.

I did. I sat in the reception area for a half hour, then an hour. After an hour-and-a-half, I decided to leave. Just as I stood up, a short, wiry, middle-aged guy—wavy brown hair, white shirt with sleeves rolled up to his elbows—walked up to me. "So what do you really know about photo-lithography, kid?"

"Everything," I exaggerated.

"Bullshit," he scoffed.

So I told him I actually had worked in a printing plant in New York and that I'd come to Texas to find steady work, get my life together and eventually save enough money to go to college. His face relaxed; he almost smiled. "I always wanted to go to college," he said, "But I never made it." He rubbed his chin. "I'll give you a week. Prove to me I should keep you around, and I will. If you don't, you're out on your ass."

"It's a deal," I said. I thanked him. "What's your name, kid?" he asked.

I straightened up to my full six-foot two-inches "Stanley Sheinbaum, sir."

He didn't bat an eye. "Henry Stamm," he said as he extended his hand. "You got one week, Stanley Sheinbaum."

When my week was up, Henry Stamm hired me full-time. Within three months I was making $50.00 per week, double what I'd ever made in New York, and the cost of living in Houston was a third of what it was in Manhattan.

Everyone I worked with in the plant was very friendly and I was often invited to go for beers after work. In most ways, I truly felt like one of the guys, but no one ever invited me to their homes and no one ever tried to set me up on dates. As a result, my social life drifted toward Houston's Jewish community which was larger than you might think because of the "Galveston Movement"—essentially, immigrant Jews following the same path that I had.

In the early 1900s, a New York rabbi, B'nai Israel's Henry Cohen, and the financier Jacob Schiff, distressed over the number of Eastern European Jews streaming into New York and living in the run-down tenements on the lower East Side, organized a plan to divert Jewish immigrant ships to Galveston where the new arrivals were more likely to fan out to other parts of the country than New York. Many traveled no further than Houston or Dallas, so there were then and are today actually a large number of Jews living in Texas. In the early 1970s, there was even a humorous country music band called Kinky Friedman and The Texas Jewboys. In 2006, Kinky also ran a somewhat satirical campaign for governor of Texas. He didn't win, but he got a small percentage of the vote and a hell of a lot of attention. Good for him.

Anyway, I hadn't been in Houston more than a week or two when I bumped into a kid I'd known in New York, Danny Rosenbloom, whose father was a dentist. The family had moved to Houston, and Danny was a student at Rice Institute, later Rice University, one of the top research universities in the country. I moved into a room in his parent's house, and when I wasn't at work (and I worked constantly to earn as much money as I could), I socialized with Danny and his friends in the upper-middle class Houston Jewish community. I really fell hard for a beautiful girl named Betty Russ, and there was another dark-haired beauty, Marie Moloff. I don't know how I remember those names except I was very happy during my days in Houston, and those girls stick in my mind like it was yesterday.

Because I was doing so well, Danny suggested I enroll at Rice. I began to believe that my dreams of a more established, meaningful life really could come true, so I paid a visit to the Rice admissions office. The admissions department assigned me to a counselor, an amiable older woman with gray hair and reading glasses perched on the end of her nose. She asked me why I was interested in Rice and I gave her an edited version of my story, adding that I would be honored to attend so prestigious a university. She smiled at that. "And your high school transcript, Mr. Sheinbaum. If you bring us a copy, what will we see?"

I knew I couldn't fudge the truth. She would get an official record anyway. "I graduated from DeWitt Clinton High School in New York with a 1.75 grade point average."

She raised her eyebrows. "On a 3-point system?"

"No, on a 5-point system."

She frowned. She rolled her eyes. Finally she burst into scornful laughter. "Is this a joke? You can't possibly be serious about Rice, Mr. Sheinbaum."

I told her how hard I would work. I begged for a chance to prove myself, just as I had with the printer. I tried everything. I even told her the story about my family losing everything in the collapse of 1929.

She held up a hand. "Stop! Please stop, Mr. Sheinbaum. I seriously doubt if you could even get into HJC with those grades."

"HJC?"

"Houston Junior College, Mr. Sheinbaum. Now please, I have work to do." She indicated the door.

When Danny's parents asked me how my interview had gone, I hemmed and hawed and mumbled that Rice wanted to see an official transcript before making a decision, but my eyes must have shown how defeated I felt. "Well, they do have a quota on Jews, you know," said Mrs. Rosenbloom as she tried to comfort me, "Our Danny was fortunate to get in." But I knew it wasn't any quota that was blocking me. It was my own miserable performance in high school. I felt that I was probably condemned to working menial jobs for the rest of my life.

Meanwhile, my life in Texas was taking place against the backdrop of a much more profound struggle, one which had not yet made significant impact on most of the Jewish community in Houston—the coming war with Germany and Japan. It's true that those of us not deeply involved in social issues, of which I am really pained to admit I was one at that time, had only heard rumors of the horrors Jews were experiencing in Germany, and Pearl Harbor was still some months away. I really have to say, in retrospect, it's hard to understand, for even me to understand, how clueless I was.

And since I'm coming clean about those war years, let me add that my military career was hardly one to provide redemption for my ignorance. I most emphatically did not single-handedly defeat the Nazis and make the world safe for democracy. In fact, I was drafted into the army in the late fall of 1941, and ordered to report on November 13, six days after Pearl Harbor. But I was so nearsighted, I failed the physical, so I went back to work at Rein's, the printing plant in Houston. Then there was a second massive call-up in the Spring of 1942, in May. The need was great, the standards were lowered, and so I entered the army and was sent to Fort Leonard Wood, Missouri.

To my surprise, my induction test scores were very high and since I was a skilled lithographer, I was slated for the United States Army Corps of Engineers, specifically the 650th Engineer Battalion, a topographic battalion, a map-making unit. So, Stanley K. Sheinbaum spent World War II as a mapmaker. Ah, well.

Actually, my army years were very good for me because they increased my confidence in myself, confidence that I could do a good job, that I got along well with people, that I was good at managing and organizing; and for the first time, I also discovered that I could be a good teacher because our unit evolved into a teaching unit which trained other units to go overseas and make maps for strategic operations.

I was eventually stationed in of all places Medford, Oregon, about as peaceful and bucolic a small town as you can imagine, just a few miles north of the California border. We were near Ashland, Oregon, where they have a famous summer Shakespeare Festival, and so I spent a lot of time in Ashland, made friends with a couple who owned a pharmacy there, dated some…well, I actually did very well with girls from the area. I was in uniform, and you know, southern Oregon is a very simple, romantic area. What's more, the place doesn't change much. I was passing through there a few years ago and saw the very same restaurant, The Mountain something or another restaurant, where I used to eat an occasional lunch fifty-five years earlier. Beautiful country.

But I would also leave Oregon from time to time, and sometimes I would go down to San Francisco where I got to know my mother's "entertainment business brothers." They were just normal guys with families who made their money running a restaurant and a small cabaret theater. Hardly the loose living, wild and crazy people my mother warned me about. They shared with me their feeling that they retained a certain affection for their sister, my mother, but that she'd always been sour, demanding and arrogant. Their stories helped me understand that I wasn't personally the cause of my mother's unhappiness…well, at least not the major cause.

It was during one of my visits with the brothers that I first visited the campus of Stanford University in the foothills of Palo Alto, just south of San Francisco. To this day, Stanford has a beautiful campus, mission-style sandy colored buildings with red tile roofs surrounded by huge trees and lush greenery. My image of a university had been the urban campuses of Columbia and NYU plopped down in the middle of New York City. I fell in love with Stanford and allowed myself the fantasy that if I ever had the chance to go to college, I would go there. It was a safe fantasy because I was sure it would never happen.

I also had the opportunity to travel around the West training other mapmaking units. I was astonished at how magnificent and varied that part of the country is: everything is so vast, massive mountains, big open skies, forests filled with giant trees. I can honestly say my view of the world which, had been entirely shaped by New York, changed radically when I was stationed in the American west and I felt thrilled and excited to experience that change in perception. Also, I suppose a little guilty. Sure, training all those other units that did go to Europe or the Pacific providing maps for the troops and the Air Corps actually was a valuable contribution to the war effort that I can look back on with some satisfaction. But I really can't take much pride in my service considering the terrible experiences other soldiers were subjected to and the Holocaust devastating Jews in Europe. However, it was during this time in the army, in my mapmaking unit, when I encountered the most terrifying incident of anti-Semitism that I have ever personally experienced.

It was actually very odd. We enlisted men lived in barracks filled with bunk beds, and I slept on a bottom bunk. A man I barely knew slept in the bunk above me. I can't even remember his whole name (it was Tom something) or if we ever had any significant interaction at all other than to nod hello or try to stay out of each other's way when we were getting ready for bed. But one night, not long after lights out, all of a sudden, out of the blue, this guy screams, "I'm gonna' kill you, you Jew Son-of-a-Bitch!" I'm half asleep, disoriented, when I realize he's jumped off the top bunk, landed next to my bed and he has his hands wrapped around my neck trying to strangle me. And he's doing a pretty damn good job of it, too!

I'm gasping for air, trying to figure out how to escape his grasp, when my right hand feels one of my boots on the floor. So I grab my steel-toed boot and start whacking this guy Tom over the head with it, whack, whack, whack as hard as I can while I'm starting to lose consciousness. But this jerk's determined. He doesn't let go of my neck. I'm passing out…and I'm thinking, what a way to die in the war!

Thankfully, our fracas raised a huge commotion in the barracks and the other soldiers came running to our bunk and pulled that asshole off of me. He did a year in the stockade, but a year later, when I was on practice maneuvers near Bend, Oregon, I got the word that Tom had been released and he was looking for me. This time I went into the woods for the night; I knew how to take care of myself in the wild by then, and by morning the military police had found him and arrested him again.

I can't say there are any profound lessons to be learned from that incident. The guy was obviously off his rocker. But yes, I guess what happened does say something about how completely irrational hatred can infect someone's brain and ruin his life…as well, of course, as the lives of the people they hate. Yeah, I guess I did take that lesson from my experience and I did use that insight to help me gain a deeper understanding of the issues confronting us when I was involved in top level Palestinian/Israeli negotiations many, many years later.

In August, 1945, I was on a Liberty ship out in the Pacific Ocean headed for the Philippines, seasick, leaning over the railing, puking my guts out, when we got word by the Armed Forces Radio Network that US planes had dropped a terrible new weapon on Hiroshima, Japan. Three days later, it was announced that a second atomic bomb was dropped on Nagasaki. Six days later, Japan surrendered. Germany had surrendered in May. World War II was over.

Given my later opposition to the Vietnam War, United States' Latin American adventures, the Middle Eastern wars, and pretty much any invasions by the United States against much smaller opponents, I'm often asked how I felt about World War II in general and the atomic bomb in particular. Since I've promised to do my best to be honest, I have to say, as an American, and yes, as a Jew, I do believe the war against German fascism, against the Nazis, was totally justified and I am proud of what my country did. I guess that war was what we would call a "just war" although it makes me nervous to use that term. I am not proud of dropping atomic bombs on Japan, but I did feel at the time, and I still do now, that it saved the lives of countless American soldiers and possibly, at least hypothetically, more Japanese lives than the bombs destroyed. I don't know. An invasion of the Japanese homeland would have been a bloody, tragic undertaking for soldiers and civilians, but nuclear devastation of a civilian population is awfully ugly, terrible, maybe unforgivable even if necessary.

I spent my last eight months of my service in Manila, Philippines, and left the army in 1946. There I was, twenty-six years old, a veteran with a skilled trade and a lot of experience, but I still wasn't established, still didn't have any sense of belonging anywhere, still with only a third-rate, high school education. After all I'd been through, I wasn't any closer to my goals than I was six years earlier when I left New York to go to Texas. Then I heard that Congress had passed what has come to be known as the GI Bill, which included the provision that the government was going to pay for a college education for any veteran who wanted to attend college. That was tremendous news. It changed everything. Finally I would have a chance to get ahead, to really make something of myself. I immediately applied to every college I could think of, including of course, Stanford, and then waited for their responses with great anticipation. They all came in, one by one, and I was rejected by each and every one.

I am definitely not given to pessimism or depression, but that was one of the darkest periods of my life. I had moved back to New York and I was living with my parents. As the rejections piled up, my mother started in on me again: "I told you so, Stanley, but you wouldn't listen to me. Now look at what's become of you," and, "Stanley, you've turned out even worse than your father." I couldn't really argue with her. I didn't know what I should do. One morning early, after listening to her over breakfast, I stormed out of the apartment and walked over to Riverbank Park, then north on Riverside Drive just walking and walking, trying to get my thoughts together. After an hour or so, I found myself at the foot of the George, the George Washington Bridge, staring up at those beautiful criss-crossed steel towers. I climbed to the sidewalk on the south side of the bridge and headed out over the Hudson River.

It was a beautiful, clear morning and my view of New York City was spectacular. I leaned against the railing, looked down into the river flowing north, so it must have been high tide. I stood there for awhile, alternately staring into the Hudson and out at the New York skyline. I was very despondent. I'm glad it was a beautiful day because I was truly feeling sorry for myself. If it had been a gray day? Who knows? Then I remembered what my father had been through, leaving his mother and father and brothers and sisters behind, coming to America, making it big and then losing everything with a wife and kids to support. My troubles were small in comparison. So what did he do? Yes, of course, he stood up and tried again, and again, and again. And that's what I had to do. I smiled just as the sun rose over the top of the Empire State Building. I had to try again.

And that's what I did. I went back to DeWitt Clinton High School as a 26-year-old, looking ridiculous, my knees too high to fit under the desk. I took, at one time, during one semester, Chem I, Chem II, Physics I and II and Trigonometry. Tough courses, and it was tough going. But I got As in all of them. With those grades on my transcript I reapplied to a number of colleges, but I still had my heart set on Stanford. Well, of course, Stanford still said no, but they offered me an interesting proposal—if I could get a year at an accredited university under my belt, and if I did exceedingly well, they would at least reconsider my application.

Then the issue was finding a college that would accept me. I was still getting rejection after rejection when one day a thicker envelope arrived from Oklahoma A & M (Agriculture and Manufacturing) in Stillwater, Oklahoma. The school has since been renamed Oklahoma State and it has an excellent reputation. But back then, I only applied because it was on a list the Veterans Administration had given me of colleges with available openings. I did know where Oklahoma was located because of my time in Texas, but I had to look up Stillwater on a map. It wasn't easy to find, stuck there in the north central part of the state, about half way between Tulsa and Oklahoma City. Basically in the middle of nowhere. But Oklahoma A & M was my only acceptance. What choice did I have? Stanley Sheinbaum, Okie! My story was getting stranger and stranger.

CHAPTER THREE
Oklahoma!

Ev'ry night my honey lamb and I sit alone and talk and watch a hawk makin' lazy circles in the sky. "Oklahoma," lyrics by Oscar Hammerstein, music by Richard Rodgers, 1943.

So there I was, finally in college, in Oklahoma, in Stillwater, in an agriculture and mechanical land grant school, in their engineering program. You may laugh. It's okay with me, but let me tell you, although Stillwater is not Palo Alto, it's also not at all like those bleak, gaunt, bitter Dorothea Lange dustbowl images so evocative of rural devastation during the Great Depression.

Stillwater is surrounded by green rolling hills, a lot of small lakes and streams, not dramatic or impressive, but really pleasant, part of the Great Prairie grasslands that dominated North America before the European settlers arrived, killed all the buffalo, and ploughed under the grass to create farms. Eastern Oklahoma was not at all what I expected, and while it's true the people were mostly whitebread, after my experiences in Houston and Medford and Ashland, I was changing my New York attitudes about heartland Americans. As long as we didn't talk religion or politics, I found middle Americans to be some of the friendliest, most open and straightforward people I've ever dealt with.

The campus of Oklahoma A & M was also a big surprise. The buildings were constructed from red brick and designed in that sort of neo-classical, Jeffersonian style one expects to see in rural Virginia. There were trees everywhere, beautiful fall foliage, and in spring the dogwoods were in bloom. One could do much, much worse than being stuck in Stillwater, Oklahoma, but I never intended to stay there for more than a year anyway. My heart was still set on Stanford, but I was curious, even I guess, a little anxious, okay, maybe even a little afraid to find out if I could handle college-level work and move on to make my place in the world.

After the first two months or so, around the beginning of November, just as the cooler weather was coming on and the winds were bringing early morning frost from the northern plains, my anxieties were resolved because I was already feeling confident about my ability to handle the work load. I had a few tests and papers under my belt, and the grades were mostly As with an occasional B to keep me on my toes. Surely those grades were the sort Stanford wanted to see.

Because I was doing so well, I was surprised when my English Composition teacher asked me to drop by her office because she wanted to talk with me about my latest paper.

As I waited outside her door, I speculated about what might be wrong. I was an army veteran and New York City boy. She was young, younger than I was, and very pretty in that fresh, scrubbed, Midwestern way with dark blonde hair and sparkling green eyes. Had I written something to offend her? Did I misunderstand the assignment? What could possibly be wrong? Her composition course was the only non-engineering course I was taking, but it was required by the university, so I simply couldn't afford to screw up. The stakes were too high. Cautiously, I knocked on her office door. She told me to come on in.

She was dressed in a plain dark gray sweater and a matching wool straight skirt. Her hair was pulled back. She looked gorgeous, sitting there behind her desk. She smiled and indicated I should sit down. "Well, Mr. Sheinbaum?" she said.

I was too nervous to respond.

"About your Twain paper." She hesitated.

I gulped. "My Twain paper?"

"Yes."

"My paper on Mark Twain?"

"Yes. Obviously. So, what did *you* think of it?"

"Uh, what did I think of it?" I knew I sounded like an idiot, but I wasn't going to take any chances and say something before I knew where this conversation was going. "Uhm, well, Mark Twain, you know, he was, uh…"

She smiled. "I thought it was very good. A+ work, Mr. Sheinbaum. You obviously know your Twain."

I didn't think I knew my Twain at all. I just picked him as a topic because he seemed to me to be so very all-American and I thought he was probably very popular at a school like Oklahoma A & M. "Well, yes, uh, thank you," I managed to get out.

"In fact, Mr. Sheinbaum, all of your papers so far have been of exceptional quality. I'm very proud of you, a veteran of the war, and going back to school when you're so much older. It must be difficult."

"Well, sometimes, yes," I was aware that something was going on. I grew more confident. "But I have big plans for my future, so I'm willing to work hard to get what I want, you know."

She smiled again. "Yes, I can see you are…willing…. Uh, could we talk more, over coffee, off campus? How about that little restaurant just off North Main near 6th Street downtown? About 4:00 this afternoon or thereabouts, Mr. Sheinbaum?"

"Sure," I said. "Sure, uh, see you then."

And so began one of the most torrid love affairs of my life. We "did it," as we used to say in those days, in her apartment, my cramped basement apartment when my roommates were gone, a small motel just outside Tulsa, in my buddy's car parked out by Boomer Lake, a cheap motel in Oklahoma City and one very nice vacation resort for three days in a row over the border in the Ozark Mountains of Arkansas. But never on campus. We never even held hands on campus.

Obviously everything was going great, and I had decided going to college was obviously the best decision I had ever made. Not only was I having the best sex I'd ever had up to that point in my life, I was able to keep my grades up as well. Then, in early spring, my teacher/girlfreind told me she wanted to take me to a reception at her grandfather's house in one of the posh suburbs of Tulsa. "Oh," she said, "and wear your uniform. It will help." Help what, I asked myself. I assumed we were going through some sort of test, but I did as she requested.

In the evening, we drove up to a very large beige sandstone house where all the lights were blazing, and there was a line of cars pulling up to the front portico. We went inside where everyone was greeted by a white-haired, distinguished looking old man and an equally white-haired handsome woman, obviously his wife. I heard numerous people refer to him as the governor, and I asked my girl who he was. "Oh, she said, "he's why we're here. He's my grandfather. He used to be the Governor of Oklahoma. Come on, I'll introduce you."

She dragged me over to the receiving line. "Grandfather, I'd like you to meet Stanley." I held out my hand and he grabbed it firmly in his.

"Nice looking young man," he said to his granddaughter, "tall…" and then noting my uniform, "and a veteran too." He turned back to me. "What did you say your last name was, son?"

I felt someone softly kick my leg, but I ignored it. "Sheinbaum, sir. Stanley K. Sheinbaum."

The governor looked toward his wife, then back toward his granddaughter. "Sheinbaum. Sheinbaum. Hmm. Where are you from, Mr. Sheinbaum?"

Again a little kick, but I remained oblivious. "New York City, sir."

"Ah, yes, of course, you would be. Stanley K. Sheinbaum from New York City." He paused. "Well you two enjoy yourselves," and then to his granddaughter, "Give your father my best. I'll call him tomorrow."

By the time we moved away from the line into the crowd, I had recovered and was becoming more aware of what had happened. I asked her, "Was that all about what I think it was about?"

"What?" she said.

"That Sheinbaum thing."

"What Sheinbaum thing?" she said.

"You know, when you kicked me, when your grandfather asked about my last name and the fact I'm from New York."

"Kicked you?"

"Look, why did you bring me here?"

"Let's not fight, Stan."

"Who's fighting? I'm not fighting."

"Come on, let's get out of here."

When we were driving back to Stillwater, I said, "I don't think your grandfather likes Jews."

"It doesn't matter," she said as she cuddled up against my shoulder.

But it did matter, and over the next few months we gradually drifted apart. Finally we did have a huge fight. I got pissed and told her I never intended to stay in that two-bit cow town anyway, that I was going to go to a real school, to Stanford University in Palo Alto, California, where I would never have to wake up in the morning to the scent of manure and wet hay ever again.

Well, that did it. We never saw each other after I said those things to her, except in class. I was worried she would give me a failing grade and kill my chances to transfer. But to her credit, she gave me an A, and so I felt somewhat badly about the whole mess. Still, I know it never would have worked. In the end, we were from two very different worlds.

My grades after a year at A & M, were so good that Stanford was more or less forced to honor their promise to admit me if I did well, so then, like tens of thousands of Okies before me, I headed off to California. My straight-A transcript gave me the confidence I could handle college work, and I was excited to face the challenges of my new life in Palo Alto.

As it turned out, Stanford was a challenge in more ways than I imagined, and the experience really did change me from a young guy who, even at twenty-eight years old, was essentially still a narrow-minded wise ass with a fairly unsophisticated outlook, into a mature man with a much broader view of the world and open to the possibilities of how I might create a productive life in that bigger world.

When I entered Stanford, I was still majoring in engineering. Because of my cultural insecurity, I held tightly to my faith that there was some sort of certainty in numbers, in precision, in mechanical things. I suppose that belief came from my father who, although he was an entrepreneur, was always very craft oriented, always working with machines and factories. That's why I chose photo-lithography over the theater. That's why I ended up in a map-making unit in the army. That's probably why I ended up at Oklahoma A & M. And even at Stanford, I was not, in the beginning, willing to let go of my faith in the practical.

However, when I arrived in Palo Alto, I was immediately exposed to students and teachers who were not primarily concerned with practical matters at all, people who cared about art and literature and politics and philosophy. They were more like my friends who went to Columbia back in New York and left me behind. Since those early days, since I left New York, I had avoided, consciously or unconsciously, spending time around people who were intellectual and sophisticated. At Stanford, it was impossible to avoid them.

I eventually began to hang out with a loosely knit collection of students, ten or twelve of us, we were labeled the not very imaginative name "the group," which was salvaged by the fact we always put the emphasis on *the*. It made us feel important. My closest friend was Al Rubin, who is still a very dear friend, one of my oldest and dearest friends sixty years later. Al became a well-known screenwriter and a major force on the board of the Writers Guild East in New York. At that time he was my political mentor for everything left of mainstream. That was necessary because I was, much to his horror, at that point in my life, very, very naive in my politics.

I remember once we were sitting and talking in a Palo Alto café, and I told him that there was this interesting old Russian guy who lived in the same boarding house where I was living, and that this Russian seemed to have been someone important when he was younger.

"What's his name," asked Al.

"I don't know, Kerenhov, Kerensky, something like that. His first name is Alexander. We talk in passing…"

Al almost fell off his chair. "Alexander Fedorovich Kerensky! You live in the same house with Alexander Fedorovich Kerensky?"

"Yeah. So…"

"Damn it, Sheinbaum, he was one of the most important, actually the most important, figure in the Russian revolution except for maybe Lenin, oh, and I guess Trotsky. He was the first Prime Minister after the revolution. Wow! This is fantastic. So what do you guys talk about?"

"Nothing much. The weather. The food. I guess I should try to spend more time with Kerensky, huh?"

I think Al almost gave up on me as a potential lefty after that conversation, but he hung in there and eventually I came to respect and understand his Marxist analysis of politics, social structure and economics. But at the time, I was simply learning all about my new world. There were so many new things.

For example, I had always been interested in music since I discovered Benny Goodman as a teenager, but many in our group at Stanford were involved with classical music and dance to which I had little or no exposure. I remember there was one dark-haired beauty who played the cello. We dated for awhile and I even took cello lessons to the point where I could play at a very basic level. Sometimes when I was alone practicing I would understand why musicians say the cello reminds them of a woman's body. I occasionally thought of my English teacher back in Oklahoma and realized I was still not entirely over her and the circumstances under which we split up. But, whatever the reasons, I did learn to appreciate classical music, especially string music, and I once shared my pleasure at learning the cello with Nathan Gardels, the Editor of New Perspectives Quarterly when I became the publisher, because I found out Nathan had actually been an accomplished cellist when he was young. And of course, much later in my life, I became a big supporter of the Los Angeles Symphony.

I also learned to appreciate ballet about which I knew absolutely nothing before I came to Stanford. Of course there's another young woman behind that story too, but those romances of my youth led me into new directions that have lasted a lifetime. In the case of ballet, I was for a while anyway, sort of the Czar of Ballet in Los Angeles when I was the chairman of the Music Center of Los Angeles County Dance Presentations. All of these cultural influences were originally born and nurtured in Palo Alto.

And yet, the most important change in my life came, as it should during university days, in my academic life. As my view of the world grew, I felt less interested in engineering and I was looking for a new focus. I still loved mathematics, and so I determined that a good mix of social science and numbers might be found in economics. That's why I decided to take Economics 101 as one of my electives during my senior year.

I was immediately enthralled, although Al Rubin kept reminding me that the Economics Department at Stanford was pretty conservative. I didn't care. At that point I was learning the basics and trying to figure out what the various economic theories were and how they evolved and who the most important economists were. Then, during the final exam, there was an essay question that must have had something to do with limits to production and cash reserves. Whatever it was, I answered the question as best I could, and after I turned in my exam, I forgot about it. A few days later, my professor, Elmer Fagan, stopped me after class.

"Are you familiar with Evsey Domar and Roy Harrod, Mr. Sheinbaum?"

I panicked. I had absolutely no idea who they were. "Not really. I think you might have mentioned them once in class. Uh, they're Keynesian economists, aren't they?"

"Very famous and important Keynesian economists, Mr. Sheinbaum. They've just published a significant book describing the Harrod-Domar model of economic growth which assumes fixed proportions in production. Interestingly enough, your argument in answer to the essay question is the basic gist of what they are arguing in their book."

"But honestly, I never…"

"I know, Sheinbaum. You may be smart, but you're not clever enough to plagiarize a brand new theory which none of us altogether understand yet. You're two-page answer can't touch their work. But you do propose some of the same reasoning."

"Thank you…I think."

"So, what are you studying, Sheinbaum?"

"Engineering."

"Engineering. Hmm. Why are you in engineering, Sheinbaum?"

"I'm here on the G.I. Bill. I need a good job."

"So…you're not going to graduate school?"

"I hadn't really thought about it, sir."

"Well, you should think about it. And you should think about economics. You seem to have a knack for it."

"But how would I…"

"There's always a way, Sheinbaum. Come see me if you're interested. We can work out a package that should get you through."

And that's how I ended up becoming an economist—one answer to an essay question that happened to catch the eye of a professor who cared.

Graduate school was truly wonderful. I became Fagan's teaching assistant and together we were quite a team. Fagan may not have been an earth-shattering economist, but he was a great, entertaining, and very effective teacher who had learned to make fun of his own bumbling, absent-minded style. He taught me how to be a dynamic instructor, how to engage student interest, how to drive home the essential points of a lecture. It's absolutely true that students used to line up on registration days to get into the economics classes that Fagan taught and I was the teaching assistant.

I was involved in serious intellectual research as well. The great Hungarian-born economist Tibor Scitovsky, Distinguished Fellow of the American Economic Association, Fellow of the Royal Economic Society, member of the American Academy of Arts and Sciences, Corresponding Fellow of the British Academy, and so on and so on and so on ad infinitum, took an interest in me. Under Scitovsky's influence I became more and more interested in international economics and international relations. I learned Russian and French, studied European economics and Marxist theory although Scitovsky hated Marx. Al Rubin was becoming damn proud of me.

During this time I also became involved, really, honestly for the first time in any serious way, in domestic politics. I was still a firmly middle-of-the-road Adlai Stevenson Democrat, and so, when election time rolled around, I walked precincts (we used to actually go into neighborhoods and knock on doors) for Senator Alan Cranston, who was a distinguished center/liberal politician in California. I also became involved in a speakers forum where we brought in conservatives and then liberals and then conservatives to try and hear all points of view —it was Stanford after all. We had Richard Nixon at the one extreme and Harry Bridges, the communist leader of the International Longshore and Warehouse Union at the other. I think Al Rubin was behind getting Harry Bridges. He was always fascinated by Harry. Many years later Rubin wrote a great screenplay about the fiery union leader, but of course, no one would make that movie.

So, just as things are rolling along nicely after three years in the Stanford graduate economics program, I was meeting with Elmer Fagan and he asked me what I was going to do next.

"Next?" I said. "I haven't even taken my orals or finished my doctoral dissertation."

"You're getting stale, Sheinbaum. Time to clean out the pipes!"

"I need to get my PhD. I need to get my career started."

"See what I mean. You started late, you're getting older and now you're in a big hurry. You need to travel. When was the last time you were in Europe?"

"Europe? I've never been to Europe."

"Well, you're going now. We'll get you a Fulbright and off you'll go. You can take your orals when you get back."

So I applied for a Fulbright Scholarship in order to finish writing my dissertation in Paris because I was writing about French-American exchange rates and currency fluctuations in the 1890s. And lo and behold, I got the scholarship.

That Fall, I landed in Paris and somehow found a small room to rent in a house on the Rue d'Anjou with a woman and her four daughters. Talk about culture shock. Stanley Sheinbaum in Paris? I wasn't sure what I was really doing there as I wandered around all the tourist sites, the Eiffel Tower, the Louvre, the Champs-Elysées, Notre Dame. My first days there were both thrilling and disorienting. I fell in love with the city. I couldn't help it. Paris is just so seductive.

So then, big surprise, I wasn't there more than a few weeks, when who do I run into in a Left Bank café but Tibor Scitovsky. He was as shocked as I was.

"So, Sheinbaum," he asked in his thick Hungarian accent, "what are you doing in Paris?"

I assured him I was working hard on my dissertation, working every day and doing research. I told him I had taken a small room with a woman and her daughters.

"Ach," said Scitovsky, "you come to Paris and live with a French woman who has four daughters and all you do is work? Please, Sheinbaum, are you crazy?" He held up his wine glass by the stem.

"What do you mean?" I asked.

"Look, Stanley, you are like a vine that has the potential to produce good wine because you have good, strong roots. But you have spent many years in fallow fields, untended, undernourished. You need to grow, develop. This is your time. Trust me. Enjoy this beautiful, beautiful city. Travel all over Europe. Soak it all in. Everything! Everyone! Now is the time, Sheinbaum. Now is the time. Take advantage of it."

Well, the four daughters were safe; they were much too young. And my landlady was so nice and kind, but very unattractive. However, I took the remaining advice from my mentor Scitovsky, and pretty much left my dissertation sitting on a small table in the *Institut de Sciences Mathématiques et Économiques Appliquées* and walked all over the City of Light before I resumed my travels.

Then the dissertation remained untouched in the institute while I rambled north throughout Holland, Denmark and Sweden, all of which had recovered from the war and already felt comfortable, even prosperous. The dissertation remained on its lonely perch as I headed back south through Germany, where I could still see the effects of the war in bombed out villages and towns, and where I had to fight off my Jewish anger and paranoia every time I heard someone yell something in harsh, clipped German. The dissertation remained undisturbed as I admired the snow-capped mountain peaks in Switzerland, ate well in Italy, took a ferry across the Adriatic into Tito's Yugoslavia, wandered down the Balkans into Greece and then took another ferry to exotic Istanbul, Turkey. The dissertation could wait. There were, after all, other daughters. And other landladies. And I had been told this was my time.

CHAPTER FOUR
The Michigan State Fight Song

On the banks of the Red Cedar, there's a school that's known to all. Its specialty is winning, and those Spartans play good ball! "The Michigan State Fight Song," lyrics by Irving Lankey and Arthur Sayles in 1919. The melody from an early American hymn, "Stand Up, Stand Up for Jesus."

When I returned to Paris and reluctantly resumed work on my dissertation, I would run into Derek Bok from time to time. He was later to become the highly respected and longterm president of Harvard University, but I knew him because we had been graduate students together at Stanford, and then we were in the same group that won Fulbrights to study in France. He married, while we were in Paris, Sissela Bok, née Myrdal, who was the daughter of the famous Swedish economist Gunnar Myrdal and the politician and diplomat Alva Myrdal, both Nobel laureates. Pierre Mendès-France, soon to become prime minister of France, officiated at their wedding, and numerous other dignitaries, such as Edgar Faure who headed up at least half a dozen ministries in postwar France, were also in attendance.

One of the wedding parties was held at the legendary Maxim's of Paris. I was a starving student, sitting amongst these extremely famous, accomplished and powerful people when that creepy old feeling that I was a nobody surfaced again, and I began to feel badly about where I was in my life—which was nowhere really. Derek's mother glanced across the table and asked me why I seemed upset when it was such a wonderful occasion amidst such beautiful surroundings. I was astonished that she even noticed me. "I...I'm fine," I said.

She persisted, so I made up some story about being worried that I couldn't get a second year Fulbright in Paris, and she said, "Oh don't worry, dear boy. We can get Gunnar and Pierre and maybe even Edgar to endorse your application. I am sure that will be sufficient."

Of course it was, and I got the second year in Paris, but despite her kindness, I really wasn't a boy anymore, dear or not, and I was pretty certain another year would not, could not, cure my ennui. Despite Fagan's and Scitovsky's encouragement and advice, I was still nervous about my future. Even my travels began to seem frivolous—essentially I was a tourist flitting from place to place, never really understanding what I was seeing, never really getting to know the people. Furthermore, my dissertation on French/American exchange rates during the 1890s didn't interest me anymore when I realized I didn't really care about French/American exchange rates during the 1890s at all, and so, try as I might, sitting at my dreary desk at the institute, I couldn't write on the subject. I just couldn't, and didn't.

Months passed, and I was becoming completely uninterested in my day-to day life in Europe. Sure, it was great to be able to participate in events like Bok's wedding. Then, my best friend Al Rubin and his wife were in Paris for awhile, and we did have fun engaging in the sort of intellectual, and probably pseudo-intellectual, discussions one is supposed to have in Paris cafés. But Al was living in London, making good money, happily married and well on his way to becoming a successful writer, while I was still living the bohemian life in Paris. I asked myself, was this really the time for me to be hanging out in Europe? I certainly didn't feel like I was getting any closer to my goals. I wasn't even sure what my goals were anymore.

That's when I decided to apply for teaching jobs back in America, and Michigan State University made me an offer I couldn't refuse, although, like the character in the movie *The Godfather*, I have often wished later that I had.

I arrived in East Lansing eager, committed and I must say, very excited. I was not only going to teach economics, but the other half of my job was to be the campus director for its Vietnam Project, a major technical assistance project under contract to the United States Department of State to aid Vietnam in agriculture, general economic development, and police training. Now, as I've said, I was definitely a middle-of-the-road Democrat who believed, as those of us in the so-called Greatest Generation mostly did in the 50s (all except my buddy, Al), that America was going to save the world. After all, we had won the war, rebuilt Europe, and were poised to rescue other nations as well. It was our task, even our destiny, as Kennedy would later declare, to bring, peace, harmony, democracy, and prosperity to the planet. *All* of the planet if possible. I truly believed that. After all, when I was traveling, I had seen the effects of the Marshall Plan on Europe. I was a full-blown optimist about America and its role in history, so I fully supported the concept of the Vietnam Project.

After I got settled in at Michigan State, it didn't take long before my part of the project was running smoothly. I recruited a number of really bright, clever students to work on various sites in Vietnam, and the Vietnamese who came to the Michigan State campus all appeared to be amazingly studious, intelligent, and able. My teaching was also going very well, and I enjoyed it immensely. Others on campus treated me as an important part of the faculty. Students in my classes were enthusiastic about the material, and they indicated they especially liked having me as their teacher. I was so glad to be working again, and I definitely had a renewed sense that my life was back on track and I was doing important things, yes, for myself, but also for my country.

My social life improved as well. Because I was the director of the project, I was often going from East Lansing to Washington D.C. to consult with government officials in the State Department, and I made it a point to travel by way of New York City so I could get back in touch with my New York friends. And then, well, one of the results of those frequent New York stopovers was that I was married for the first time. Out of the blue. Just like that. And I do not tell you this as an insult to her, but I can barely remember who she was, and I absolutely cannot remember why we decided to get married. Strange isn't it?

Okay, I do remember a little more than that. Her name was Lynn Bloom, but as I try to reconstruct the series of events that led to that marriage, nothing comes to mind. We must have dated at least a few times. Where did we go? I must have found her attractive, but I don't remember what she looked like, or that I was overwhelmed with desire. I can only assume that I must have considered a wife to be a necessary accoutrement in order to be truly accepted as a successful man.

Now I'm not very proud to say that. In fact I'm ashamed to say it, but why else would I have married a woman I clearly didn't love and can barely remember? I don't believe we actually fought with each other until just before the marriage ended. I think that maybe after our initial fascination, we probably avoided each other and didn't communicate at all. I may have also been so busy I never had enough time for her. I was teaching and also traveling a great deal, working very hard to make sure the Vietnam project was a success.

My responsibilities as head of the on-campus project eventually required that I travel to Saigon so I could get a better perspective on how our on-campus training was coordinating with the in-country operations. I was also excited to go to Asia, where I had never been, and I was looking forward to seeing our operation there and the people I had recruited to work in Vietnam.

However, despite my enthusiasm, things started out badly, and I felt a sense of foreboding before I even left the States. An assistant from the office of the president of the University stopped by to brief me on my trip. He had with him a man from the US State Department who I'd never met before. They both treated me as if I were a minor functionary and made references to the fact that the project was "much bigger, more important than any of the individuals who worked for it." Of course their admonitions could have meant many things, so I didn't want to overreact, but they bothered me.

Those were the days before intercontinental air travel by jet, so the flight on a turbo-prop aircraft was loud, long and exhausting. Then, when we landed in Saigon, the weather was hot, humid, and sticky. The streets were flooded with people, bicycles flying by left and right and the constant drone of those smokey little two-cycle motor scooters assaulted my ears and the smell from their oily exhaust was unbearable. I didn't sleep well at night. There was no air conditioning, and I was not in the best of moods; in fact, I was down right irritable.

On the day when I was being given a tour of our facility by the head of the Vietnamese end of the project, we slogged through a muddy demonstration field where I was shown that we were developing new varieties of rice to create larger yields. We were clearly doing good work, but the mud and the heat made for a miserable experience. I felt better after an excellent Vietnamese lunch, and then we decided on a visit to our headquarters building. I passed through two or three classrooms where Americans were tutoring Vietnamese on how to implement the basic structures of Western capitalist economic theory. Then, as we approached the stairwell which led up to the fifth floor of the building, I couldn't help but notice that we ignored the stairs and instead proceeded on down the hall. "What's up there?" I asked as I pointed toward the fifth floor.

My guide shrugged. "Oh nothing. Just more classrooms."

"What are we teaching on that floor?"

He became more evasive. "Uh, I'm not sure exactly."

"Can I at least have a look?"

"I would have to check and see."

His attitude seemed strange to me. I was getting very annoyed. "Look," I said, "I'm the Michigan State campus director for this project. Why shouldn't I be able to go where I want and see what I want?" I headed for the stairway.

"Mr. Sheinbaum, Professor Sheinbaum, you can't go up there. Please, it's the policing part of the project. There's heavy security." I kept moving up the stairs. "Please, Mr. Sheinbaum, the door will be locked. You can't get in."

I'd had it. I exploded, "The hell I can't," I said. I reached the door to the fifth floor and grabbed the handle. My guide was right. It was locked. I knocked on the door. There was no response. I banged harder. After a few moments of my continued banging, a burly figure opened the door but blocked my entrance. He looked at me menacingly. "You can't come in here," he growled.

Well, I'm a pretty big guy myself, so I huffed and puffed and threw back my shoulders and said, "You can't tell me where I can or cannot go. I'm your damn boss, buddy."

My stance didn't phase him. "You're not *my* damn boss," he spat. "Now clear out, whoever the hell you are…Now!"

By that point, my guide had caught up with me. "Please, Professor Sheinbaum. Let's see the rest of the project. You don't need to be on the fifth floor right now."

I considered my options, took a deep breath and calmed down. "Okay, okay, but I want an explanation. I need to know what this is all about."

After that experience, I started asking the sort of questions I probably should have been asking from the beginning. I'd been too starry-eyed; I'd been too taken in by the project's success and my own pride. I sought out one of the Vietnamese students I had known fairly well when he studied in East Lansing. I knew he was connected with the police training so I hoped I would get some straight answers. I asked him why everything on the fifth floor was so secret.

"We have to have good security. There are Communists everywhere."

"Communists?"

"Yes," he said, "revolutionaries. Communists from the north. And Buddhists here from the south. Our own people. There are enemies everywhere. They want to overthrow the government."

"Is that a police matter?"

"Yes, of course. We must keep control."

"Of what?"

"The country. The people. Everything, Professor Sheinbaum. Your people tell us we must know everything, control everything."

"My people?"

"Yes…your government people, your CIA people."

"CIA? What CIA people?"

He seemed perplexed. "The ones on the fifth floor, Professor Sheinbaum."

It became clear to me after a few more discreet and not-so-discreet probing interviews that the policing part of the project in Vietnam proper was being run by the CIA, and that they were dealing in counter-insurgency, torture, intimidation of the populace, police undercover infiltration of Buddhist organizations, and government control of the media and pro-government propaganda.

I was shocked. Really, I was. I suddenly realized my project wasn't exactly about promoting democracy; we were instead a cover for the United States government to prop up an anti-democratic South Vietnamese regime. Okay, keeping it real, at that time I honestly might have been able to accept some of that activity on the part of my government "to stop the Communist threat," but I could not come to terms with the fact that our supposedly college-administered aid project was working secretly with the CIA to create and manage a puppet government under the cover of Michigan State University. This seemed to me to be against the very principles we were supposed to be promoting.

When I got back to East Lansing, I asked for an interview with John Hannah, the president of Michigan State and a legendary figure. Hannah had built the university from a small regional college into a nationally recognized research institution. He had also taken the school from an enrollment of 15,000 to almost 40,000, and he was aggressive and adept at developing government contracts. I knew I was meeting with a powerhouse, but I also believed, naively I guess, that his position as one of America's leading university presidents would make him sympathetic with the proper relationship between academia and counter-intelligence.

Hannah's office was that of a typically uber-masculine CEO meant to impress and intimidate—dark paneling, heavy drapery, book-lined walls, large full windows overlooking the leafy campus. It worked. I was impressed and intimidated. So, I began by expressing how much I appreciated teaching and working at Michigan State and how much my life had improved since I started working there. Hannah nodded. Then

I began an explanation of how I had discovered that the CIA was heavily involved in the Vietnam Project and…

Hannah interrupted. "I thought you said you were pleased to be here in East Lansing and that you enjoy your work here. Did I hear you correctly, Sheinbaum?"

"Yes, of course, sir," I replied. "But…"

"You know, Mr. Sheinbaum, what you're telling me is really none of your business."

"But sir, I'm the campus director for the project."

"That's correct," said Hannah, "and that's *all* you are."

"Okay…but is it appropriate for an academic…"

Hannah was losing his patience. "As I said, this is none of your business. You're here to manage the project on campus. I am told you are doing a good job. I would suggest you continue to do a good job and not ask too many questions about matters that don't concern you. If you're bored, *Mr.* Sheinbaum…by the way, it is *mister* isn't it? You still don't have your doctorate do you? Well then, why don't you get to work on finishing your dissertation? Then maybe someday you can run a major research institution and make the important decisions. In the meanwhile, if you are not happy here, or your curiosity just overwhelms you, I am prepared to accept your resignation, *Mr.* Sheinbaum." He then made it clear our discussion was over.

So that was that. I had to make a decision: to stand up for what I was convinced was the absolutely correct moral position and end my academic career just as it was getting off the ground, or continue to run the project as I had been doing and not ask any more questions.

I talked to a number of people about what I should do. One day I was certain I should leave, the next day that I should stay. At some point I had a long talk with someone, it may have been my left-wing conscience, my old buddy Al, but I'm actually not sure. Whoever it was, he reminded me that we, the United States, through Michigan State University, were propping up a totally corrupt South Vietnamese government headed by an ineffective puppet, Ngo Dinh Diem, whom we had installed to do our bidding. Our entire involvement, both the government's and the university's, was going to blow up in our faces at some point and, at a minimum, the project would be disgraced. With that conversation in mind, I decided to resign.

Now, at the time I said nothing publicly, but a few years later, working with the investigative journalist Robert Scheer on a long article for *Ramparts* magazine, he and I did expose Michigan State's involvement with the CIA in Vietnam, and I explained how that involvement helped to lay the groundwork for an ever greater US commitment to propping up the failed South Vietnamese government which eventually led to the quagmire which we now know as the Vietnam War. More about that later, but the *Ramparts* revelations did ensnare President John Hannah and he was eventually forced to resign as president of the university.

I must admit I viewed Hannah's downfall with a certain *schadenfreude*. Interestingly, he was immediately appointed head of the USAID (The United States Agency for International Development) so his sympathies and loyalties concerning our government's international involvements became rather obvious. On the other hand, I do have to give him credit for being the first chairman of the United States Commission on Civil Rights, so domestically, there are many things to be said in his favor.

Meanwhile, I was unemployed. This obviously didn't sit very well with Lynn, still my wife at the time. I think her comments more or less parroted those of my mother thirty years earlier, starting with: "You're an idiot, Stanley."

"I just couldn't go on living a lie like that, Lynn. It wasn't right."

"So what are you going to do now?"

"I don't know. I'll find something. We'll be all right."

"Well," she said, "*I'll* be all right for sure. I'm going back to New York. Alone. Good-bye and good luck. You're a real loser, Stanley K. Sheinbaum."

I pretended I didn't care what she said, but her words stung me, and of course the pain was multiplied because I had heard them before.

After I left East Lansing, I went back to New York to try to finish my dissertation at the National Bureau of Economic Research, a highly respected place which is primarily tasked with analyzing business cycles, but talk about boring! I couldn't believe I had gone through experience at Michigan State only to end up in another uninteresting, dead-end situation in a gray anonymous bureaucracy. I was becoming convinced that the humorous expression, "no good deed goes unpunished" might actually be true: Stand up for what you believe in and lose your job, lose your wife, and end up living a meaningless existence.

All in all, I was getting pretty good at feeling sorry for myself when one day the phone rang and the voice at the other end said, "Hello, this is Robert Maynard Hutchins."

Well, I knew who Hutchins was. Everyone in academia did in those days. He was a very influential educational philosopher, the highly respected ex-dean of Yale Law School at age twenty-eight, and president of the University of Chicago when he was thirty. Then he left Chicago to head up the Ford Foundation, and I could not think of any conceivable reason why Hutchins would be calling me. So I figured it was one of my smart-ass friends trying to fool me. I laughed and responded, "Yeah sure, and this is John Maynard Keynes."

The voice then said, "No you're not. I knew Keynes. But this *is* Hutchins. Would you like to talk to me or would you rather not?"

I recovered as quickly as I could. "Of course. I'd be honored to talk with you, Dr. Hutchins."

"Well then, would you like to come to California and work with me?"

"Are you kidding? Of course I would."

Well, it turned out that Hutchins was leaving the Ford Foundation and developing a think tank of his own—a center that would focus on educational philosophy as it applied to the development of democratic institutions. This concept eventually evolved into the influential Center for the Study of Democratic Institutions in Santa Barbara, California. One of the men who was helping Hutchins gather fellows for the Center was Carl Stover who was a graduate student with me at Stanford. Stover knew about my experiences at Michigan State and suggested to Hutchins that I might make an interesting addition to the group of permanent fellows. So I went out to California for an interview.

I remember the very first time I went through the Center's front door, a very elderly man was leaving and he said to me, "Hi, I'm Reiny Niebuhr." It was Reinhold Niebuhr, one of America's pre-eminent ethical theologians who is still quoted by everyone from Jimmy Cater to John McCain to Barack Obama. Okay, I was just processing that I had spoken with Reinhold Niebuhr when I decided I better stop by the restroom before my interview. It was the old-fashioned open restroom where men urinate in a common area, and as I'm standing there, a voice behind me booms out, "Mind if I join you?" I glanced at the man speaking to me, and it was Chief Justice of the Supreme Court William O. Douglas who was to eventually become chairman of the board at the Center.

Needless to say, by the time I entered the conference room for my interview I was completely anxious, but I assume I must have done all right. Hutchins asked me a number of questions about the Vietnam Project, and Wilbur H. "Ping" Ferry, an economist who had been with Hutchins at the Ford Foundation grilled me pretty hard over my credentials as an academic economist. But in the end, I think Hutchins liked me. He remembered our phone call and he seemed amused by the incident. You know, good things often hang by very thin threads, and a few weeks later, I received a formal invitation to join the Center, which I accepted with no reservations whatsoever.

The Center really changed my life in many important ways. For one thing, participating in roundtable discussions with minds like Niebuhr; Paul Tillich, another theologian; the founder of the American Democratic Socialist Party, Michael Harrington; the Pulitzer Prize winning writer Harry Ashmore; Justice Douglas; US Senator Kenneth Keating; New Jersey Governor Clifford Case (I think that's enough name dropping for the moment), really gave me the confidence I could hold my own anywhere with anybody. But the most important single event that happened to me while I was at the Center, happened while I was attending a party in Los Angeles. I met the woman who would unalterably change my life forever, my second and really only wife, my life partner in all things, my best friend and confidante, the truly amazing artist and political activist, Betty Warner Sheinbaum.

CHAPTER FIVE
I've Heard That Song Before

It seems to me I've heard that song before. It's from an old familiar score; I know it well..."I've Heard that Song Before," lyrics by Sammy Cahn, music by Jule Styne, 1942.

You would think that after all the turmoil at Michigan State and my long struggle to overcome my insecurities and establish myself as a successful, respected man, I must have been delighted to have landed a position as a fellow at the Center for the Study of Democratic Institutions, which, at the time, was one of the most influential think tanks in America. And you'd be right. I was delighted! And I was thankful. The Center was the final rung in the ladder I had been climbing, the place where I discovered my confidence in my ability to debate and discuss ideas with powerful minds and profound individuals who included if I remember correctly, in addition to those names I've already dropped in the previous chapter, the Catholic theologian Father John Courtney Murray; Adolf Berle, a member of FDR's "brain trust" and author of *The Modern Corporation and Private Property*—a groundbreaking work on corporate governance; Stringfellow Barr, President of St. John's University and co-founder of it's unique Great Books program; education philosopher Frederick Mayer (*A History of Educational Thought*); Linus Pauling, one of the most important scientists of the 20th Century; Bishop James A. Pike, an Anglican theologian; Robert Kurt Woetzel, international law expert and one of the first proponents of a World Criminal Court; Harvey Wheeler, the influential political scientist who co-authored *Fail-Safe*—one of the first novels to illustrate the horrors of nuclear warfare; Alexander Comfort, later to attain fame as the author of *The Joy of Sex*; the French philosopher and futurist Bertrand de Jouvenel; and Stanford biologist Paul R. Ehrlich, author of *The Population Bomb*. There were many, many others, and in the process of interacting with them, I was able to develop confidence that I could play in the big leagues.

And I genuinely liked Robert Hutchins. He was, arguably, the most intelligent man I've ever met and he was also attractive, personable, articulate, and possessed of a very clear, focused vision of who he was, of where he was going and what he wanted to do. He was, in all, a very impressive person. And at the beginning of my time at the Center, when I was still very tentative around those daunting intellectuals, Hutchins was very supportive.

As it turned out, Hutchins, like me, was an early riser who preferred to be at his desk before the daily routine of meetings and discussions began. When I walked into the charming old Montecito estate that housed the Center, my office was down a hallway on the far left, but Hutchins was usually in his office, immediately to the right of the entrance. We would often have coffee and schmooze about the news, baseball scores, politics, other personalities at the Center, whatever was on our minds. One day, after a few of these sessions, when we had become comfortable with each other, he asked me, "Sheinbaum, what is your problem in the discussion groups?"

"Problem?"

"You're awfully quiet. Here in my office, you talk nonstop, but in our group meetings, you seldom utter a word."

I thought about what he said. "Well, I guess, you know, it's a very impressive group. I'm not sure how I fit in."

"You fit in however you make yourself fit in. It's a heady, scholarly atmosphere here, but also very competitive. You have to make your mark. No one is going to hold out a hand and invite you to participate."

"In the discussions about economics?"

"Not just economics, maybe not even primarily economics. I am interested in you, Sheinbaum, because at Michigan State you were involved in many issues beyond economic theories. For example, you took a strong stand for keeping politics out of the academy. I feel the same way."

"Well, that involved the CIA."

"True, but I feel that way about all electoral politics, not only intelligence agencies. I believe that in a democratic society, the university, academia, should be a place for study, debate, and discussion removed from the concerns of everyday affairs. That is the environment I want to preserve here at the Center, and that's why I wanted you to join us."

Hutchins' encouragement gave me the confidence to become a more aggressive, involved fellow, but, as I was to find out before too long, his philosophy that electoral politics had no place in academia was a double-edged sword that eventually became a weapon used against me and the direction my life was taking.

If the Center for the Study of Democratic Institutions was my final training ground for interacting with powerful people, I have to admit what those who know about my later life will be surprised to discover, that at forty years old, I still didn't have a clear, focused set of political values. Sure, with my newly developed talents and my greatly increased confidence, I was finally ready to go out into the world and make my mark, but where? How? And most important, why? I definitely didn't want to become one of those men who are clever and bright just for the sake of being seen as clever and bright. I needed to feel committed. I wanted to be where the action was. And as I look back on those times, I realize that two factors, more or less extraneous to the Center, were pulling me toward a more activist, involved life, a committed life. The first was my marriage to Betty. The second was the Vietnam War.

Betty Warner was a child of Hollywood, the daughter of the legendary mogul Harry Warner, one of the brothers who founded Warner Bros. Studios and the president of the studio until 1956. At a relatively young age, Betty married a successful screenwriter and producer, Milton Sperling, and they had four children: Susan (later known as Desiree), Karen, Cass and Matthew. Betty and Milton also had a long history of being involved in left/progressive political causes, and Betty was, in her own right, an artist as well—a hard-working, dedicated sculptor and painter.

I was introduced to Betty at a party in Los Angeles hosted by her friend. Betty's marriage was already on shaky ground, and I later found out her friend introduced us because she thought Betty and I would hit it off and the friend was considering putting the moves on Betty's husband if Betty was out of the picture. Well, Betty and I did hit it off, but Betty's friend didn't get Milton. He married a younger European woman none of us even knew about. Sometimes life works out like that.

I remember I was immediately drawn to Betty, not just because she was beautiful, but because she was so passionate about life, politics, and ideas. She hated the Hollywood life. She wanted to be involved with places like the Center and people like Robert Hutchins and I guess, men like me. When I first met her, at her friend's party, I remember she was holding some sort of drink in her hand when she looked up at me, she was much shorter than I was, and asked me what causes really mattered to me. I was momentarily taken aback. I wasn't used to someone being so aggressive about ideas and causes at a party. For a moment, she reminded me a little of my old lefty friend Al Rubin.

"Uh…uh, well, Vietnam, the war, for example. I'm worried about our involvement there." I told her about my experiences at Michigan State running the Vietnam Project and then how and why I resigned. I hoped that would impress her.

It didn't. "So you resigned, Stanley. That's great, but what did you really do about exposing the CIA involvement with Michigan State?"

"Well…"

"And what are you doing now? What are you doing about our involvement in Vietnam?" Her eyes sparkled. She was serious but also having fun with me.

"Uh…uh, at the Center we…"

"No, Stanley Sheinbaum, what are *you* doing? Don't you think you should commit to *doing* something, not just talking about it, not just analyzing the issues?"

Suddenly, everything was clear to me. "Yes," I said, "I do think I should get involved and do something. Yes. You're right. I really do."

She touched my arm, and leaned into me. "Good man. I like men who act on their convictions."

Well, I was smitten. But there were complications. Betty was still married to Milton and there were the four kids. I liked the kids, really, I did, but I'm a bachelor at heart, not a family man, and I knew I could never be a good father to them. I am sorry about it, but I really wasn't a particularly good stepfather. I wasn't exactly a bad stepfather either, I just, well, my relationship with my own mother and father and brothers was so alienated, so strained, I didn't know how to create a close loving family relationship.

And then there was the money. Betty inherited, as you can imagine, a lot of money. I had no money to speak of. I determined that the money was a problem we had to work out. Not so much for Betty, but for me. I was uncomfortable with all that money.

It seems that in every lengthy interview I have ever given, the issue of Betty's money comes up, and I usually steer the conversation toward the fact that I made, at one point, some very shrewd currency arbitrage decisions that increased the value of Betty's estate considerably, so in a sense, I contributed significantly to our wealth. I also emphasize that Betty and I have always used the money not for personal luxuries but to support progressive causes with humanitarian values. But always in the final printed interview, the underlying accusation creeps in that it's easy to be progressive and liberal and even support socialist ideals if you're sitting on a big pile of money. The same accusations haunt George Soros who also has made a ton of money on currency fluctuations—far, far more, by the way, than I ever did.

Anyway, after we'd been together for awhile, Betty and I were sitting in the yard on a perfect Montecito afternoon when the golden sun filtered through the gnarled branches of the huge old live oak trees and a cool breeze blew in from the Pacific Ocean. I must have been in my grumpy mood, because Betty asked me what was wrong.

"I'm just tired," I said.

"You always say you're tired when something bothers you."

"Okay, it's about the money," I said.

"We don't have money problems, Stanley. We are very fortunate. We have more than enough money."

"But that is the problem. Look at me lying here doing nothing on our beautiful property on a perfect Montecito afternoon. Disgusting."

"Disgusting?" Betty exhaled. She was, I think, more than a little bit annoyed. "Look, Stanley, the money…well, my money, now our money, and I want it to be *our* money from now on, can give us the freedom to do the good things we believe in, to act rather than just talk, talk, talk like so many of our friends do, to genuinely help people and causes we believe in. That's how I see our money."

"But we didn't earn it."

"No, we didn't. That's true, but one of the reasons I fell in love with you, aside from the fact that you're so clever and handsome," that twinkle in her eyes again, "is that you do want to be involved. I can see in you a fierce determination, that once you focus on an issue, you won't let go. You're the kind of guy that will make things happen. And our money will give us the freedom to commit to those causes we think are important. I want the rest of our lives together to be centered around those struggles. That's the kind of life I want to live. I think that's the kind of life you also want to live, isn't it, Stanley?"

I thought about what she said the rest of the afternoon and into the evening. I woke up during the night and thought about what she said again. I realized Betty, out of love, was providing me with the psychic armor neither my mother nor any other woman had ever given me. It was difficult to accept her gift. The feeling was new to me, but once I understood how fortunate I was, I never looked back, and I never felt guilty again. Lucky, but not guilty.

The cause that first tested my determination to get involved was of course the cause with which I was most familiar and to which I had already taken tentative steps and made some small sacrifices—the ever escalating war in Vietnam.

As the war in Vietnam fades in America's collective memory and Vietnam becomes better known to the majority of Americans as the country where our tables and chairs and shirts and pants and athletic shoes are made, it becomes increasingly difficult to explain why the Vietnam War disillusioned so many Americans. That disillusionment was particularly bitter because the United States had not long before, during and after WWII, created a system of alliances with Western Europe and Japan that dictated that democratic capitalism was the dominant political and economic hegemony. As a result, we Americans were admired and envied by most of the world. So what went wrong? Rather than go into a lengthy explanation, let me just throw out statistics we tend to forget: almost 60,000 American soldiers were killed and hundreds of thousands injured, roughly three million Vietnamese dead, our own country torn apart by assassinations and civil disruptions unlike any we had seen since the bitter labor strife of the early 1900s. Many would argue that the cultural divide and the severe political turmoil experienced in the United States today, well into the 21st Century, is more or less a direct result of the chasms that developed during those Vietnam War years. So, for me, who very early on in the conflict, had been humiliated and shocked to realize I was an unwitting front for the CIA, ending the war in Vietnam became my chosen battleground.

Although the Center was not at all left wing, and in fact, although Hutchins did oppose the Vietnam War, he worked very hard to stick by his principles and keep the Center out of electoral politics. He was determined to avoid having the Center associated with active opposition to the war. But this was the '60s, and all sorts of radicals, from Mario Savio, who became famous at Berkeley for the Free Speech Movement—which threw the University of California campus into complete turmoil—to the left-wing labor journalist Paul Jacobs, approached the Center for the Study of Democratic Institutions trying to get Hutchins to support their causes. Hutchins wouldn't even meet with them, so leftists often ended up finding a sympathetic ear in me.

As a result of these meetings, I went up to Berkeley from time to time. On one of those occasions, Jacobs introduced me to a brash young journalist named Robert Scheer. We met in an empty parking lot, and I was told the point of meeting in the lot was to make sure our conversation wasn't being recorded by one government organization or another. I thought Scheer and Jacobs were being a little paranoid, but years later when I learned that Woodward and Bernstein met Deep Throat in a parking lot, so, well, maybe Scheer knew something I didn't.

Scheer was extremely curious about the Vietnam Project at Michigan State.

"Why is that so important?" I asked him.

"Not important," he remarked rather forcefully, "essential, Sheinbaum. Don't you get it? That's where it all began. Your Wesley Fishel who ran the Michigan State team over there in Vietnam single handedly picked Ngo Dinh Diem to be the puppet president of South Vietnam."

"Fishel did?"

Scheer just shook his head. "Even though you were part of the system, you still don't quite understand how things were do you, Sheinbaum? Look, just give me everything you know. I'll connect the dots. We're going to blow this whole corrupt scenario wide open."

Despite, or maybe because of his impatient, aggressive attitude, I liked the young guy, and so I did give Scheer everything I knew. Then, I even arranged for the first version of our story to be published by the Center in pamphlet form titled, *How The United States Got Involved in Vietnam*. Hutchins was not pleased. Neither was Harry Ashmore who was already maneuvering to take over the Center when Hutchins gave up the reins. Later on, a more complete version of Michigan State's involvement was printed in *Ramparts* magazine. That story garnered national attention and launched Scheer's career as a major American journalist whose interviews for *New Times, Ramparts*, and later *Playboy* eventually led to his becoming a writer with the *Los Angeles Times* where eleven of his stories were submitted for Pulitzer Prize consideration. He also became one of my very best friends.

Meanwhile, my situation at the Center was getting somewhat strained. It wasn't just me, all the fellows were aligning into two camps, one led by Harry Ashmore who wanted to avoid involvement in the controversial issues around the war and street protests, and the other coalescing around me, urging the Center to get more involved. The situation was exacerbated by Hutchins' failing health. Our early morning chats, once so warm and friendly, were less frequent. Often Hutchins wasn't in his office at all. One morning we did meet and after shooting the breeze for awhile, Hutchins finally asked me why I thought it was so important that the Center get involved in anti-war efforts.

"Because the Vietnam War is becoming the issue around which all other issues are debated," I argued.

"But, Stanley, I don't want the Center involved in these hot button topics. We will lose perspective about what's truly important. How we preserve the integrity of democratic institutions and make them even more powerful. that's what matters in the long run."

"But if we don't get involved, the Center is in danger of losing touch with the evolving intellectual movements of our times. We'll be seen as irrelevant. You read what the *New York Times* wrote about us."

I could see the hurt in Hutchins' eyes. I could feel his pain. He was silent for a moment or so. "I guess I really am getting old," he finally mumbled.

I didn't mean to be cruel, but I pressed my point. "We're all getting older, sir. That same article named me as the youngest fellow at the Center and I'm in my mid-forties."

More silence, then, "Well, you may be right, Sheinbaum, but I founded this Center as a place for contemplative thought and intellectual speculation. If things come to a battle, I won't be on your side."

I was sad to hear him say that because I realized our friendship was ending and I owed him and the Center so very, very much. I really did. What's more, I didn't actually want to get involved in the internal politics of the Center. Once Betty and I had teamed up, my situation allowed me the freedom to act independently. However, I wasn't ready to cut off all my ties with Hutchins and the other fellows, so I suggested that I become part-time, and that eased the tensions somewhat.

Not long after I went part-time at the Center, I read an article in the *Los Angeles Times* that indicated that the US Air Force wanted to bomb Cambodia because the North Vietnamese supply lines, the infamous Ho Chi Minh Trail, supposedly ran through Ratanakiri Province in northeastern Cambodia. I knew immediately that investigating this information (which I believed to be false) was important, and I no longer felt I had to hesitate out of any loyalty to the Center. I immediately called Scheer. "Pack your bags," I told him, "we're going to Cambodia to check out this Ho Chi Minh Trail story. I don't think it's true. I think the government just wants to expand the war into all of Southeast Asia."

"Sounds good to me," said Scheer, and off we went.

When we arrived in Phnom Penh, we met with a representative of Prince Norodom Sihanouk, Cambodia's head of government, and convinced him to help us get to the northeast of the country to find out what was going on. After a few days of negotiations, he agreed to help, and by coincidence, or as far as I know it was a coincidence, the Australian ambassador who looked after US interests in Cambodia, since the US had no formal relations with Sihanouk's government, wanted to go to Ratanakiri as well. So we all jumped into Cambodian military trucks and then onto a government plane and traveled together to the border with Vietnam.

Now, to this day, I'm not certain why the ambassador came with us, but his presence turned out to be quite fortuitous. Scheer managed to talk him into appearing in many of the photographs we were taking of the border areas, and so, it was clear the photos were taken in Cambodia, not Central Park, New York, or Griffith Park, Los Angeles because the Australian ambassador was in the pictures. And it was also clear there were no bridges over the ravines and gullies. No bridges meant no trail. No trail—no reason to be bombing Cambodia. We got what we came for and could prove it beyond our expectations.

In fact, we were in such a good mood about our investigation and the results that, on the way back to the States, I decided to stop in Vietnam where my youngest brother Gilbert Sheinbaum, who had become an official in the State Department, was stationed as a special assistant to Ellsworth Bunker, then the US Ambassador to Vietnam. I wanted to talk to him about the war. I wanted to show him what we had discovered about the non-existent trail in Cambodia. And, I wanted to convince him that our policy was a disaster. Instead, it was my visit that turned into a disaster.

After a few hours, Gilbert and I could barely stand to be in the same room with each other. "Stanley, listen to me. Who cares if the Ho Chi Minh Trail exists or not? Who cares if Cambodia gets dragged into this? We have to stop the Communists here or the whole of Southeast Asia will fall!" He shouted, red-faced and angry. "This is part of the world-wide struggle to stop the Communist menace."

I shouted back at him. "How can we stop Communism and promote democratic capitalism by backing a totally corrupt, undemocratic bunch of scoundrels?"

"So you want the Communists to win, Stanley. You think, like mother always said, you know everything, don't you, Stanley? So you would undercut the efforts of your own country to make the world a better place because you think you know more than we do here in the embassy?"

"Our Vietnam policy is making the world a worse place. We're not the good guys anymore, Gil. We're the bad guys."

"You arrogant commie pinko!"

"Government bureaucratic hack!" I stormed out the door, and Scheer and I caught a plane back to the States.

Gil and I are now friends again, but for many, many years we didn't talk at all. That's how bitter things became, even within families, during those Vietnam War days.

When I got back to the States, I went to see Senator William Fulbright, chairman of the Senate Foreign Relations Committee and the very same man who had created the scholarship program that sent me to Paris back in the 50s. He was also known to oppose the Vietnam War, so I presented our evidence to him and argued that the Air Force's request to bomb Cambodia was a scam. He believed me, and he used my information to hold off the bombing for another three years, but of course, eventually the United States did bomb Cambodia, which did bring Cambodia into the war, which then led to the disastrous Pol Pot regime and the horrors of the Cambodian genocide. But I did what I could, and I was proud of what I was able to accomplish simply by getting involved.

As the war continued to escalate, Scheer and I discussed various strategies to raise the public's consciousness about what was happening in Southeast Asia. Finally we each decided to run for Congress in the Democratic primaries; he did so in Berkeley and I ran in Santa Barbara. We were both among the first candidates in the country to challenge the Democratic leadership on the war in Vietnam.

I discussed my decision with Betty and she was in complete agreement. She teased me, "I always wanted to be married to a congressman."

"I doubt you'll get your wish, I said. "I'm only running to raise awareness about the war. I don't think there's the proverbial snowball's chance in hell that I can win."

"You're probably right," she said, "but it's no fun going into the race with the attitude we can't win. Let's say we can win and see what happens."

So we entered the race with as much optimism as we could muster. After all, there was a new spirit sweeping across the land and we were determined to be an important part of it. As it turned out, we were.

(left) Stanley (l) and his older brother, Herbert, in Riverside Park, NYC.

(right) Stanley and his younger brother, Gilbert, in the Bronx, NYC.

(left) The Sheinbaums (l-r) Selma, Stanley, Herman, Herbert and Gilbert (front), after moving back to Manhattan.

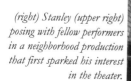

(right) Stanley (upper right) posing with fellow performers in a neighborhood production that first sparked his interest in the theater.

(left) Sergeant Stanley Sheinbaum near Medford, Oregon.

(right)Stanley hovering over a light table in the map creation room.

Stanley (center, right near wrench) and his map-making buddies taking a break to pose in the pine forests of southern Oregon.

(left) Stanley with his mother, Selma, and his father, Herbert. His parents did travel to Palo Alto to attend Stanley's graduation from Stanford.

(right) Stanley leads a graduate seminar in economics at Michigan State.

Stanley (far right) with Robert Scheer (far left) and an unidentified Vietnamese police officer (in uniform) and an intelligence officer (white shirt).

(left) Stanley in Cambodia, which he first visited when he was the campus director for the Michigan State Vietnam Project.

(right) Stanley greets newly arrived Vietnamese students slated to participate in the Michigan State Vietnam Project.

(left) Stanley meeting with other members of Michigan State Vietnam Project around the time he became suspicious the project was a CIA front.

(left) Stanley (center) and Robert Maynard Hutchins (foreground) participate in a conference at the Center for the Study of Democratic Institutions in Santa Barbara, California.

(right, l, to r.) Stanley, Harry Ashmore, Supreme Court Justice William O. Douglas and Robert Hutchins remark on the Center's progress during a break from a legal seminar held at the Santa Barbara Biltmore Hotel (photo: Hal Boucher).

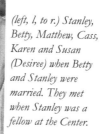

(left, l, to r.) Stanley, Betty, Matthew, Cass, Karen and Susan (Desiree) when Betty and Stanley were married. They met when Stanley was a fellow at the Center.

(left, l -r.) Harry Ashmore, Robert Hutchins and Stanley disembark at Ben Gurion Airoport during 1961 trip to Israel. (foreground) Ms. Vesta Hutchins

(right) Betty, Stanley and a very large dog during a stop in Poland during a trip when they volunteered to chaperone a group of international leadership students.

(left, l. to r.) Stanley, with the philanthropists W.H. "Ping" Ferry and Carol Bernstein Ferry, and Betty Warner Sheinbaum at the Center for the Study of Democratic Institutions.

CHAPTER SIX
Stormy Monday

They call it stormy Monday, but Tuesday's just as bad....Lord have mercy, lord have mercy on me. "Stormy Monday," lyrics and music by Earl Hines, Billy Eckstine, Bob Crowder, 1942.

Bob Scheer ran against incumbent Congressman Jeffrey Cohelen in the 1966 Democratic Congressional primary in Berkeley. Since I was living in Santa Barbara, if I won the Democratic primary, I would have had to run against the incumbent Congressman Charles McKevett Teague; good Ol' Charlie, a self-described man of the people, born and raised in the farming community of Santa Paula; good Ol' Charlie Teague whose folksy style made even Ronald Reagan seem stiff and formal. The people around Santa Barbara loved Charlie, and in 1966, the district was not only heavily Republican but also overwhelmingly in favor of the Vietnam War. And I was running a single-issue candidacy —I was against the Vietnam War. That's why I ran. That's what I cared about.

What's more, the Democrats in the Santa Barbara area weren't exactly wild about my anti-war campaign either. After all, with Lyndon Johnson in the White House and Democrats in the majority in Congress, the Vietnam War was in fact a "Democratic War" in 1966— supported by nearly as many Democrats as Republicans. This was the time before Senator Eugene McCarthy announced he would run against Johnson, before Bobby Kennedy announced he would run, before the North Vietnamese Tet Offensive in January, 1968—when the polls first began to show a massive shift in American public opinion from pro-Vietnam War to anti-Vietnam War. In 1966, Scheer and I, as well as a few others, were truly Demosthenes standing alone on the shore speaking out over the roar of the waves crashing on the beach with no one listening.

Last, even though I had become a part-time fellow, my campaign was frowned upon by Hutchins and many of the other fellows at the Center for the Study of Democratic Institutions, especially Harry Ashmore. To be fair, those opposing my campaign weren't necessarily in favor of the war, but they were firmly convinced that the Center should stand above the fray and remain a place for study, debate, and reflection. In retrospect, I understand this feeling was also linked to a fear that the Center was beginning to acquire a (totally undeserved) reputation as a left-leaning institution, and that my political involvements had the potential to endanger the Center's non-profit status.

But Betty and I were committed, so we blindly, boldly, and somewhat comically headed into the campaign trying to run it ourselves although neither of us had any experience whatsoever running a political campaign. And we were running in one of the more bizarre districts in the country: it snakes along a narrow strip more than 150 miles long down the Pacific coast from north of Hearst Castle at San Simeon through the tourist town of Cambria, more resort areas near Morro Bay, into the middle-class neighborhoods of San Luis Obispo, the agricultural lands around Santa Maria, along Vandenberg Air Force Base, winding through all of Santa Barbara and its suburbs, then into Ventura County, including the cities of Ventura and Oxnard near the northwestern edge of Los Angeles County. Running a candidate for Congress in this district is a challenge for even the most professional campaign.

Of course, if we were going to spend money and invest considerable time and effort, we wanted to make it the kind of community organizing campaign that could educate as many people as possible about the war. We decided we were not only going to shake-up the area and the Democratic party, we were going to change the community's perception of what was really going on in Vietnam. So we had intimate evenings in people's houses over coffee and cookies where we could discuss the issues, and many of these people became life-long friends. Slowly but surely, we were making headway by influencing neighbors, civic groups and student organizations. I believe it was my commitment and Betty's passion that changed so many people's minds.

But the campaign was also often unintentionally funny because we still had to go through the motions that all campaigns require. About three months into the campaign, we were finally able to get one labor endorsement, from the civil rights leader and union activist César Chávez's United Farm Workers. So, we scheduled an appearance before a couple dozen farm workers in a strawberry field outside Santa Maria. We were even able to get local TV news coverage and a handful of reporters from regional newspapers. We asked César to try and get as many of the farm workers who were going to be there to be able to speak and understand some English so when I spoke, we would get responses from the crowd which would look good for the cameras and impress the reporters.

Well, the big day dawns, I'm making my speech, and I'm a fairly articulate speaker, but I notice the crowd is amazingly unenthusiastic. There are few cheers, little clapping. I'm getting very nervous, and even though it was early in the morning and still cool, I was beginning to sweat. I stumbled through my remarks, feeling more foolish each minute, and finally I just cut the speech short and walked back to the car with Betty and César. When we were in the car heading for Santa Maria, I said to César, "I guess my remarks on the war weren't what they wanted to hear."

"Oh no," said César, "your remarks were very inspiring, Stanley."

I was silent for a moment, thinking. "Well, then, I guess most of them didn't understand English, " I said, a little annoyed.

"Oh no," said César, "most of them understood English..." He hesitated, trying to control a growing grin on his usually serious face.

"Okay," I said, "what's so funny?"

"Well...they just couldn't understand *your* English, Stanley." César said, referring to my heavy New York accent.

At first I was taken aback, then I began to laugh, Betty joined me and eventually we were all caught up in the irony of what had happened even though I was the butt of the joke. But then things turned ugly. Very ugly.

There was a group of absolutely nutty right-wingers in Santa Barbara in those days. They had even purchased a fully operational Sherman tank and parked it at the beach "to repel Communist invaders," although I'm not sure where these invaders were supposed to come from since North Vietnam had no deep-water navy, but I suppose people like that don't need a rational reason. These nut cakes left Betty and me alone until it looked like our campaign was becoming effective; then, one night, after I left for a campaign rally, Betty received a nasty hate call warning her, "Always watch your back because you and your commie husband are dead, lady." Frightened, she went to the front of the house and gently pulled back the curtain a bit. She saw a large black car roaring up and down in front of our house. At that point she was getting very nervous and upset, as she should have been, but when shots rang out and one of our front windows exploded in a hail of broken glass shards, she ducked onto the floor trembling. Moments later, there was a knock at the door. Thinking it was the police, Betty crawled over to answer the door, opened it and there was a large man wearing a dark balaclava ski mask, which only revealed his burning eyes.

"Stop the campaign you fucking Hollywood pinko Jew bitch," a voice growled. Then he turned and ran toward the black car which squealed away into the distance. When Betty finally reached me, (that was before cell phones,) I was furious and demanded that the police act, but they were never able to establish for certain who had threatened us.

One would, I suppose, also assume from the anti-semitism of that creep's remark that the Santa Barbara Jewish community supported us. (Yes, even in those days there was one synagogue.) But when I was allowed to speak to them, suddenly, in the middle of my presentation, the rabbi stood up and started screaming, literally screaming, "You dirty rat traitor to America! You commie bastard!" He was soon joined by others in the congregation hurling insults and filthy invective. Betty and I were forced to leave underneath thunderous shouting and applause that we were exiting the building. That's the way things were in the '60s once the Vietnam War became controversial. People took sides with a passion not seen again until the Tea Party upheavals after President Obama was elected. It was awful.

Although we definitely raised the community's consciousness about the war, we were resigned to the fact that we would lose the election itself. However, we were not even able to make it out of the primary campaign which we lost to a centrist Democrat. That was difficult for us to accept. However we decided right then that the campaign itself had been effective at raising people's awareness, and if our government continued to pursue the war, we would campaign again in 1968, hire professional help and make a real run at winning. We were that committed.

Meanwhile there was a new issue just over the horizon that helped erase some of the bitter aftertaste of the '66 election loss. In fact, the adventure became one of my favorite projects, a real spy caper complete with code names and very real death threats. It started with the arrest and detention of my friend, Andreas Papandreou, in a coup by a Greek military junta in the spring of 1967.

Andreas was a Greek economist and Socialist politician whose father, George, was prime minister of Greece in 1963; Andreas was himself to become prime minister in 1981; and his son, also named George after his grandfather, would eventually become prime minister of Greece in 2009.

Andreas had been in trouble with the right wing before. He fled to the United States at the beginning of World War II when the Fascist Metaxas dictatorship exiled him from Greece. He received his doctorate in economics from Harvard, taught at the University of Minnesota and Northwestern University, and then became the chair of the Economics Department at the University of California, Berkeley, which was how I came to know him; he made various presentations on economics at the Center for the Study of Democratic Institutions while I was a fellow there. He also became an American citizen and married an American, Margaret Chant, better known to me as Maggie.

Betty and I were planning a trip through the eastern Mediterranean with intentions to stay with the Papandreous at their rustic seaside home in Kastri when we heard on the radio that the junta had taken control of Greece. Concerned, we checked with the Papandreous to make sure we should still come to see them. We received word back that everything was fine and they were looking forward to our visit. Then a few days later, I received a phone call from Maggie. She was upset, frightened, near panic. Andreas had been arrested by the junta, charged with treason and thrown into prison. She asked if I could help.

I immediately hopped on a plane and flew to Greece to meet with Maggie and get the lay of the land. After conferring with numerous people and talking things over, I realized the situation was very, very serious, but there was little if anything I could do there in Greece. I didn't know anyone. I had no power or influence. "You have to go back to America and get the government to do something, Stanley. You don't know these junta people," she said, nervously, her hands shaking, tears welling up, although she didn't cry. "It's not like America, they will kill him. You have to help him, Stan. You just have to."

That evening, before I left, I went with Maggie to a road that ran alongside the forbidding walls and brooding barred windows of the old stone prison where Andreas was being held. By pre-arranged signal, Andreas was to be standing at a window at exactly 9:55 p.m. We were out on the road. Maggie intended to light a candle to let Andreas know she was thinking of him and doing all that she could to get him out of there. At 9:54 we tried to light a match, but it was breezy. The match flickered out. We tried again. Again the breeze snuffed out the match. It was already 9:55. At 9:56, we got the match to light the candle and we stood there in the night silently facing the darkened windows. Later we found out Andreas did see the light, and it gave him comfort and strength to carry on despite the guards' rough questioning and threats.

When I returned to America, I found that a group of economists, very prominent economists, had organized a committee to free Andreas Papandreou. The committee included John Kenneth Galbraith (twice a winner of the Presidential Medal of Freedom and later US Ambassador to India); Paul Samuelson (the first American to win the Nobel Prize for Economics); Kenneth Arrow (soon to be another Nobel Prize winner in 1972); (Leo Hurwicz who would, at 90, become the oldest person to win a Nobel); and in some ways, most important, Walter Heller who had been Chairman of the Council of Economic Advisors under President Kennedy and who was an extremely influential advisor to President Lyndon Johnson. I was sure this group could move our government to action. But I was naïve.

President Johnson's foreign policy was becoming more and more obsessed with anti-Communism and the Vietnam War. The Greek junta's coup, which may or may not have been aided by the CIA, certainly received relatively sympathetic winks from the American government. And the committee of economists, while raising their voices and making a bit of a stink, was, because of the government relationships of many of the members, generally unwilling to take on or even endorse any serious direct action. I quickly became disenchanted.

Then there was a break. Walter Heller made a trip to Europe on another matter entirely, but suddenly he called me from Paris. "Stanley," he said, "I've been contacted by these two Greeks who say they are the junta's primary witnesses whose testimonies will lead to the probable indictment against Papandreou."

I was obviously excited. "What have they told you, Walter?"

"Ummm, look, Stanley, I can't talk to these guys. I'm too close to the administration. I need someone who's an independent agent."

I grunted. "You mean, like me for instance?"

"Yeah, like you for instance, Stanley. Can you come over here to Paris and talk to these guys and see how credible their story is?"

So I booked a flight on the next plane for Paris, set myself up in the Paris Hilton, and met with the two Greeks, publisher Kyriakos Diakogiannis and a lawyer, Andreas Vachliotis. We met on Monday,

Tuesday, and Wednesday. I had a tape recorder running hidden under the couch. In the evenings, I'd replay the tapes and figure out how I felt about their story, which was that the KIP (the Greek CIA) had coerced their false testimony under extreme duress. On Thursday, I pretended I was sick and couldn't meet with them. Instead I flew off to Athens and met with Maggie, who gathered together contacts she could trust and we discussed what Diakogiannis and Vachliotis had told me. The consensus of the group was that they couldn't know if the testimony was given under duress or not, but yes, they all agreed those two guys were the lynchpins of the junta's case against Andreas. So I flew back to Paris and told Diakogiannis and Vachliotis that I would get them into the States and we would tell their story to the world. What I didn't tell them was that I had absolutely no idea how I was going to do that.

Since I was not sure I could trust those two and I had no way of knowing what the junta knew or what the US government knew, I didn't want to fly directly to New York. I decided the three of us would meet again in Montreal as if we were tourists visiting Expo '67, the glittering World's Fair being held on an island in the St. Lawrence River; and, if they would agree to meet me there, I would tape their stories openly and then we would drive over the border into the States.

As I look back on it, I'm telling you I really felt like I was replaying the scene from *The Third Man,* where Joseph Cotten is talking with Orson Wells as they ride Vienna's famous ferris wheel, the *Wiener Riesenrad* in Prater Park, except we three were walking around Expo 67 with that huge Buckminster Fuller geodesic dome in the background. I asked a lot of questions, and their stories seemed to hold up. I asked Diakogiannis, the older of the two, a balding man with fierce eyes and a salt and pepper full beard, why, after betraying Papandreou, were they now telling me what they claimed was their true story.

"We feel bad," he said. "We just want to set things right. Andreas is a good man."

"I'm sorry" I told Diakogiannis, "Andreas is a good man, but that answer doesn't ring true. What do you really want?"

Diakogiannis hesitated. Vachliotis spoke up, "Asylum," he said. "We want to leave Greece."

"I can't offer that," I said. "There are those I can talk to who will do what they can for you, but I cannot promise the United States will let you stay there."

"You're a smooth operator, Stanley K. Sheinbaum," Diakogiannis said. "You'll come up with something."

Well, first of all I had to get them to the Bay area, so we drove across the border and headed for San Francisco, where I housed them, fed them and generally took care of them while Bob Scheer and I talked to Adam Hochschild, who was then writing for *Ramparts* before he became a co-founder of *Mother Jones*. Hochschild agreed to write the article, and he interviewed the two Greeks for several months to get their story.

Meanwhile I was in constant contact with Maggie Papandreou. In the spirit of the operation, we had begun using code names when we communicated. She was "Joan," I can't remember why, and I was "Maynard" in honor of my ongoing allegiance to Keynes. My main concern was finding out when the junta was going to bring down an indictment against Andreas because we needed to know if their case was in fact primarily based on the testimony of Diakogiannis and Vachliotis. If not, then we were screwed because our revelations wouldn't discredit the junta's allegations against Andreas.

Months passed, and still there was no indictment. Hochschild's article was finished. *Ramparts* had set aside space in the upcoming issue. The editors were screaming at me. Hochschild was screaming at me. I think even Scheer was pissed, but what could I do?

Finally one night after Betty and I had gone to bed, there was a call. Groggy, I picked up. A voice said, "Maynard?"

"Yeah," I said. "Joan?"

"Good news, Maynard, our friend's indictment was announced this morning!"

"Based on the stories from our friends?"

"Almost entirely."

You can ask Betty if you don't believe me, but after I hung up the phone, I literally stood and jumped up and down on the bed, yelling and shouting, "We're in business! We're a go! We're in business!"

We published Hochschild's article entitled "The Framing of Andreas Papandreou" in the October 1967 issue of *Ramparts,* and we followed the publication up with a major press conference in Washington, where Diakogiannis and Vachliotis told their story to the press. Within the month, Andreas Papandreou was released from prison and exiled to Sweden. I flew to Stockholm, we embraced warmly, and he thanked me profusely for all that I had done to secure his release. He also introduced me to many of the major figures in the Swedish government which years later was an invaluable asset during the Middle East Peace negotiations in Oslo. But that's another story entirely.

To complete Papandreou's story, after that first year, Andreas left Sweden for Canada where he taught economics at York University in Toronto until his exile ended in 1974 when the junta fell. What a glorious day! Andreas insisted that Betty and I fly with the family for their homecoming after so many years in exile. He arranged to have his plane pick us up in California, and we then flew to Toronto where we met Andreas and Maggie. When our flight finally landed in Athens, the airport was overwhelmed by an enormous, totally raucous crowd (by some estimates up to one million people) cheering and chanting and calling out Papandreou's name. As Andreas left the plane, a rowdy group of Greek men grabbed him, lifted him up on their shoulders and carried him through the swirling crowd. Men as well as women were crying. The noise was incredible. The excitement palpable. Betty and I were jostled about, but we finally caught up with Andreas at the car that was to take him to his family home.

Papandreou was laughing. "They got my wallet," he said. "but what a day, what a wonderful, wonderful day."

"Well I guess somebody has a very special souvenir," I commented. We were all very, very happy and so gratified that after all those years, some measure of satisfaction had been returned to Andreas and his family.

Later, in 1981, Papandreou was elected prime minister and during the following years his administration dramatically altered the social structure of Greece to provide for a much fairer distribution of wealth and opportunity. We remained close friends until he died in 1996, and I read a eulogy at his funeral. But more important for my life story, the Papandreou episode taught me that I could be a significant player in international affairs even though I was acting on my own because my very independence gave me the freedom that official representatives can never have. I was to treasure that revelation many times over in the coming years.

Dealing with Papandreou also made me even more aware of the corrosive effects of the US involvement in Vietnam. In many parts of the world, like Greece for example, far from Southeast Asia indeed, the United States was coming to be viewed as an enemy of democracy rather than its greatest champion. And these feelings were being expressed even by people like Andreas, who was educated in America and was an American citizen. Although I, too, shared this fear about my country, the fact that people in other countries felt that way discomfited me a great deal. I wanted to be proud of the United States, and I simply did not, and still do not, believe that most Americans want us to support corrupt regimes that act to oppress the struggles of the common man to have justice and greater opportunity.

The Papandreou operation was over and I was back in Santa Barbara determined to run for Congress again against good Ol' Charlie Teague and to try once again to get people to understand how misguided and destructive the war was. Then, in November 1967, Senator Eugene McCarthy declared his candidacy to run in the Democratic primaries against Lyndon Johnson. The war was clearly getting even more controversial in mainstream America. In January 1968, there was the Tet offensive I mentioned earlier. In April, Martin Luther King was assassinated. Then urban insurrections broke out in more than 110 US cities with extremely serious upheavals and loss of life in Washington D.C., Chicago and Baltimore. It was a terrible time, the worst of times. And there I was trying to run for Congress in a district where most of the inhabitants were absolutely terrified by what was going on in the cities. Don't forget that tank on the beach!

So there I was, once-upon-a-time middle-of-the-road Democrat Stanley K. Sheinbaum, thinking about withdrawing from the race and instead doing something radical that would galvanize people to direct action. When I talked to Betty she asked what I had in mind.

"I'm not sure," I said, "but there must be something dramatic we can do to get through to people. I feel like the country's falling apart."

"All the more reason to try and change the system by going to Washington, Stanley. Hey, I didn't marry a quitter. Let's give it all we've got and see what happens."

So that's what we decided to do.

CHAPTER SEVEN
Those Were The Days, My Friend

Those were the days, my friend. We thought they'd never end. We'd sing and dance forever and a day. "Those Were The Days My Friend," credited to Gene Raskin, who put English lyrics to the Russian song "Dorogoi dlinnoyu" written by Boris Fomin with words by the poet Konstantin Podrevskii, 1925.

After so many years of struggle, self-doubt, difficult study. and constant reassessing of myself, after so many years of working hard to create a life that allowed me to contribute something significant to the world, finally, there I was at the beginning of 1968, absolutely flush with success after getting Andreas Papandreou out of prison and saving his life. I was very proud of what I had been able to accomplish. I can honestly say that for the first time I was confident I could do anything; but what's that saying from the Biblical prophets, not that I'm particularly knowledgeable about the prophets? Oh yes, "Pride goes before a fall," or something like that. I was to find that at the age of forty-eight, I was still learning who I was and what my special set of skills were. I was also to find that the Papandreou victory should have pointed out the path I would eventually follow, but I had committed to again run for Congress, so I was determined to succeed despite the warning signals.

First, I had to win the Democratic primary, and I had an opponent, Jim Horwitz, who was basically a good guy, also against the Vietnam War, and the only thing that really separated us was that we backed different Democrats at the national level—Jim was the Bobby Kennedy candidate and I was the Eugene McCarthy candidate, which actually led to one of the more humorous episodes of the primary.

Bobby Kennedy came to the Santa Barbara area to campaign since he was running in California against McCarthy and Hubert Humphrey for the Democratic presidential nomination. One week before the primary, Bobby Kennedy was touring Oxnard, and I wanted to get my car with banners on each side which read "Sheinbaum for Congress" into the Kennedy motorcade. I was standing next to my car when Dick Tuck, the infamous Democratic trickster who was forever infuriating Republicans, made one of his very infrequent mistakes by assuming I was the Kennedy candidate and telling me I should, "…go on up and sit in the convertible with Bobby and Ethel." Which I gladly did.

So the motorcade was traveling through the streets of Oxnard and we're waving to the crowds. I was chuckling inside and having a grand old time, especially since I was reminded of my ride with Al Smith so many years earlier in New York. Suddenly the car stopped at the courthouse, and there was Jim Horwitz in a crowd of reporters. He was furious to see me in the car with Kennedy. Justifiably so, I might add. But what could he do at that point? So as he's standing there fuming, the motorcade started up again and off we went to finish the parade.

When we arrived at the Oxnard Air Force Base where Kennedy was to board his plane to fly up north to close out his campaign in Oregon, we said good-bye. He stepped onto his plane and I remained in the car waiting to be driven to where I left my car. Abruptly, Bobby appeared again at his plane's door searching the crowd. Finally he spotted me. He came back over to the car and I was convinced the shit was going to hit the fan.

Bobby said, "Dick Tuck tells me you're the McCarthy man."

I grinned sheepishly. "Yeah."

Bobby broke into one of those patented Kennedy smiles. "Well done, Sheinbaum. I would have tried the same thing." Then he turned back to the plane and was gone.

Well, of course the sad part of this story is that he really was gone. Exactly one week later, as I was sitting in the Santa Barbara courthouse while the returns were tallied and I was getting ready to celebrate my victory in the primary, a hush came over the crowd as the networks flashed the news that Kennedy had been assassinated at the Ambassador Hotel in Los Angeles, and of course, I was never to see that smile again.

Those were such sad, sad, terrible days. My very good friend Paul Schrade, an official with the United Auto Workers Union, was standing next to Kennedy at the Ambassador Hotel, and he also received a bullet wound to his head. Paul survived, but he was still recovering in the hospital when I went to Chicago for the national convention—that disastrous Chicago convention.

President Lyndon Johnson was a Democrat, and although he decided not to run in 1968 for another term, the fury of the anti-Vietnam War protests were directed against the Democratic Party. There was tear gas in the streets and in the International Amphitheater where the delegates were meeting. There were police riots against the anti-war protesters in Lincoln Park. Bashed, bloody heads. Arrests. Dozens of wounded. There were even brawls on the floor of the convention itself. My sympathies were completely with my friend Tom Hayden and the other anti-war protesters out on the streets, but I couldn't bring myself to join the more raucous groups.

Betty and I did walk with a small group for one of the quiet, subdued protests near the band shell in Grant Park. Many of the people around us were worn down and weary, exhausted from street battles the previous evening. Others, like us, just wanted to make a statement that we were in sympathy. Then, even though our group was totally utterly peaceful, suddenly we heard the pop, pop of the tear gas canisters being fired from police guns. Clouds of the stinging, nauseous gas wafted across us. My eyes were blurred. I couldn't see anything. Betty was coughing and bent over. We broke ranks, somehow managed to cross Michigan Avenue where we entered the lobby of a hotel filled with other conventioneers. Small amounts of tear gas from across the way seeped into the lobby. Guests were rubbing their eyes and heading for the elevators. I put my arm around Betty's shoulder and asked her if she was all right.

"I think so," she said, but I need a minute to just sit." I looked around and sniffed the air. The smell of the gas was dissipating. I decided we were safe in the lobby itself, so we settled onto a plush couch near the registration desk. We just sat there, holding hands, not really talking, in shock at what had happened to us, which was nothing, really, compared to what others had endured and were still going through back in the park. Needless to say, the convention was a disaster that disgraced the Democratic Party, and the proceedings were televised live all over the world.

When we were back in Santa Barbara, I knew the chaos at the convention and my well-known views about the war might be difficult obstacles to overcome with the wider electorate. Furthermore, since Hubert Humphrey, the Happy Warrior and a Johnson loyalist, was nominated to carry the Democratic banner into the national election, his candidacy also didn't help me with Democrats in Southern California who were increasingly becoming anti-war. I also knew from my experience in the primary that I had to broaden my appeal to include issues I had neglected previously like income inequality, the environment and immigration. We needed professional help so I hired two somewhat experienced campaign staffers, Walter Dallenbach and Jonathan Reynolds from the McCarthy campaign. Once the convention nominated Humphrey, they were able to come to Santa Barbara and work with me. We also had numerous young volunteers, some of whom stayed with us at our house, and their enthusiasm brought a great deal of energy to the campaign.

I have to say I think I was great talking to college kids and church groups and community organizations. I was frankly less successful talking to blue-collar Democrats whose votes I really needed. Sure, I talked about income disparity, how even then, the cycle was starting where the rich were getting richer and the working classes poorer. I lamented the demise of organized labor, but phrases like "the demise of organized labor" which came easily to me, weren't especially effective when talking to factory workers. And my New York City accent along with my obviously Jewish name and my thick heavy glasses didn't exactly create magic with the factory crowd. Dallenbach would organize meet-and-greets outside manufacturing plants. I was honestly enthusiastic to try and make those meetings effective, but I could see the workers eyes glaze over as I extended my hand, and said, "Hi, I'm Stanley K. Sheinbaum and I'd like to be your Congressman." They were clearly skeptical about the prospect. Suffice to say, I was no glad-handing good 'ol boy like Charlie Teague. I just never got the hang of it.

Still, my numbers were improving each week and we were gaining traction against Charlie. I remember fondly one gimmick when we worked with César Chávez again. This time when I met with the farm workers, I talked about immigration and better wages which was much more effective. Best of all, I did so at one of Charlie Teague's family farms. That got the media out!

When our little entourage showed up early that morning on the edge of a damp spinach field, one of Teague's foremen lumbered over and told me to get the hell out of there.

"Why," I asked. "we're just talking to these farm workers who are on break."

The man glowered. "This is private property."

I pretended ignorance for the camera. "Oh really. Whose property is it?"

"You damn well know this farm belongs to Mr. Teague, Sheinbaum. Now get the hell off his land or I'll call the sheriff."

I was tempted to let him do that, but we had accomplished what we wanted to accomplish for the cameras, so we left, but we did make the evening news.

As our polling numbers continued to go up, things got nasty again. There were the threats, the intimidation, hate calls to Betty at our home. Teague went on TV and called me a commie and said I'd been an organizer for the protests at the Democratic convention. He said I was a traitor and that I wasn't a real American anyway, snidely implying that no real American could possibly be from New York City with a name like Sheinbaum. Still, I fought back, and the increasingly unpopular war became an albatross around Teague's neck not mine. Nevertheless, his accusations managed to stick with some people. In particular, the accusations of disloyalty hurt my campaign and so my numbers leveled off. I was in trouble because Charlie was eventually able to make *me* the issue, whereas I was doing my damnedest to make ideas the issue. Not only was I unable to effectively do that, I also realized, maybe for the first time, how much electoral campaigns are about personalities. And I didn't really like being the issue. It made me extremely uncomfortable.

We fought up until the last days, and I developed a fantasy that in the end we were going to pull it off. Dallenbach and Reynolds secretly agreed not to disabuse me of that notion to my face. It was kind of them. We were in the car heading for the traditional vote counting at the county courthouse when the first results were announced on the radio. Teague had a big, big lead. And those were the urban precincts where I hoped to do well. My jaw dropped. I was genuinely surprised. In the end I lost 65% to 35%, not the showing I had hoped for. It was a real downer although I was pleased that I had won the actual City of Santa Barbara precincts.

What went wrong? I now realize, nothing really. We had accomplished everything we originally hoped to accomplish: we made the US conduct of the war a legitimate question in people's minds, initiated awareness about the plight of undocumented immigrants long before they became a national concern, focused on the environmental impact of oil drilling off the beautiful Santa Barbara coastline, and raised alarms about the growing income inequities between the rich and the poor. Those were the things that Betty and I cared about, and I believe we initiated a change of attitude in the Santa Barbara area that developed and grew so that today the community is a far, far more progressive, involved and caring place than it was in the '60s.

What was wrong, or what felt wrong, is that I didn't fit into that community anymore, at least as a politician, as a public figure. If I ran for office, I would always, personally, be the issue, and I carried a lot of baggage in an area like Santa Barbara. Clearly, I was very controversial no matter what I did. I had also outgrown my position as a fellow at the Center for the Study of Democratic Institutions, and anyway, Hutchins was retiring and my nemesis, Harry Ashmore, was slated to be the new director. It was time for me to move on.

After the campaign ended, I spent much of my time traveling around the country speaking on college campuses against the war. I enjoyed doing so, and being around young people lifted my spirits. I also enjoyed being back on the East Coast when I spoke to students at colleges and universities there. And I felt a powerful nostalgia for New York City which still had a significant grip on my imagination. It was my home after all, and I had always wanted to test the waters there once I had some successes under my belt. So I told Betty how I felt.

Well Betty, the working artist and art connoisseur Betty, had always been drawn to the New York art scene, but Betty was also a California girl and she loved living in Santa Barbara.

"I really love being in New York," she said. "It is the center of the art world now and the cultural opportunities are fantastic. But it's so crowded, no sense of space like here in the West."

"It's not just the center of the art world, Betty, New York's the center of the whole world. If we also want to try to make a difference in politics and the ideas that capture public imagination, we need to be in New York."

"Don't forget your family's still there."

"I've thought about that."

We continued to weigh the pros and cons, and after numerous long discussions we agreed the excitement of living in New York was simply too attractive to pass up. Ironically, it was that move to New York which ultimately led to our return to California, to Los Angeles where we've lived ever since. But that journey required a few years to unfold.

Once we were settled in the city, Betty opened a gallery on Madison Avenue and I set about making contacts. I was able to meet a lot of people in a very short time, initially through our close contacts back in California. It was through one of Betty's Hollywood friends that I met my most influential mentor and a man to whom I am eternally indebted, Arthur Krim. It was Arthur who showed me how to stop being concerned with my personal advancement and use my ability to interact with all sorts of people in order to bring them together and make things happen.

To begin with, Arthur Krim's resume was impressive. When I met him, he had been the finance chairman for the Democratic Party, an adviser to President Lyndon Johnson and the former chairman of Eagle-Lion Films. He was at that time the chairman of United Artists, and he was eventually to end his storied career as the chairman of Orion Pictures until shortly before his death in 1994. He was married to the equally accomplished Dr. Mathilde Krim, a world-renowned research scientist who later in life was awarded the Presidential Medal of Freedom. Even so, they were not particularly public figures, and if they were in the public eye at all it was for throwing Jack Kennedy's famous 45th birthday party attended by a host of celebrities including Marilyn Monroe, Maria Callas, Jack Benny and Harry Belafonte. Krim's spacious townhouse was the perfect nexus for the political, social, business and entertainment elite.

Arthur and Mathilde took a liking to Betty and me, and brought us into their lives without hesitation. I was amazed. Eventually Arthur even gave me a key to their house and I came and went whenever I wished without needing an invitation. At different times I met more Hollywood actors than I ever had back in California. I remember Gregory Peck and Burt Lancaster. Although Betty had this love/hate relationship with Hollywood after being raised as the daughter of a Warner brother, I have to admit I was fascinated to meet these people. At first, it was exciting because they were famous movie stars, but eventually I came to understand that, more importantly, they were essential components of the Krim's political and social life.

One evening Arthur and I were talking after dinner in his library, and I asked him how he juggled these different types of people.

"I don't have to juggle them, Stanley. They juggle themselves." He smiled.

I was perplexed.

"Look, Stanley," he continued, "the political people want to meet the glamorous Hollywood people and the Hollywood people want to meet the influential political people and everyone wants to meet the rich business people."

"But they meet at your place, at your parties. You are the center of the circle."

"I would venture a guess, Stanley, that most of the people you have met here while coming and going do not think of me as the center. Actors and politicians, for example, always think of themselves as the center of everything. And the rich just want to hang out with actors and politicians." He laughed. "But Mathilde and I try to never be the center of attention. Every party, every fundraiser, every event honors someone other than Arthur and Mathilde Krim. We are the go-betweens for many of these people and we always try to remain in the background."

I thought about what he was telling me. "So you wouldn't run for office?"

"No. Why would I? I would just be one officeholder. Right now, there are many officeholders who hold their positions because I helped put them there."

"You wouldn't want, just once, to put yourself in one of your studio's movies?

"Heavens no. Not even as a walk-on."

"The president of a major university?"

"Our contributions to the top research universities here and abroad give me much wider influence within academia than a university president has."

"Hmmm."

"What I'm telling you, Stanley, is that some of us, and I include you in our group, are made to work more or less behind the scenes to bring many different sorts of people to the table to make things happen. Hopefully, among progressive people like us, to make good things happen. And our efforts often go unknown and unappreciated, at least by the media and the public at large. That lack of personal recognition gives us more, not less power and influence. You told me once you did things for your friend Papandreou that Walter Heller couldn't do because he was directly connected to the government and too well-known."

"Yeah," I said, "that's true."

"Well," Arthur smiled. "You've already learned an important lesson, Stanley: you will be more successful at getting things done if most people have never heard of you. Need I say more?"

Approximately a year after my conversation with Arthur took place, I had a chance to test his advice. On June 13, 1971, excerpts from an intelligence report which came to be known as the *Pentagon Papers* were published in the *New York Times* and subsequently, the *Washington Post*. The information in the excerpts—covering the US involvement in Vietnam from 1949 through 1967—was really nothing new to those of us who were aware of how the war had developed. However, when Daniel Ellsberg, one of the Defense Department whiz kids who worked for another brilliant but totally misguided man, Defense Secretary Robert McNamara, had, without authorization, secreted the reports out of the Pentagon and turned them over to the *Times,* their publication created an uproar.

Since the excerpts contained no information that could reasonably be considered matters of national security, the *Times* clearly felt it was their journalistic obligation to publish the material to enlighten the general public as to how the country got into the mess the Vietnam War had become. The Nixon Administration, which had taken ownership of the war after Nixon had defeated Humphrey in '68, was furious, outraged and determined to prosecute Daniel Ellsberg for leaking what they considered classified information. In many ways, the *Pentagon Papers* controversy paralleled the *WikiLeaks* revelations about the Iraq and Afghanistan wars some forty years later.

Personally, the issues around the Pentagon Papers meshed perfectly with my anti-war sentiments. At the time, I was still traveling around the country speaking, mostly in academic circles, against the war, and I was pretty well known as an activist. So when Ellsberg was arrested and it became clear that the government was going to prosecute him, I volunteered to organize the legal defense team and raise the money to pay for Ellsberg's defense.

Initially, my activities were centered in New York and Washington where the controversy first broke into the open. I contacted two of the most prominent civil liberties attorneys in the United States. The first was Leonard Boudin who had represented Dr. Benjamin Spock, the famous baby doctor who advocated draft resistance during the war. Boudin had also represented other well-known anti-war activists including the civil rights organizer Julian Bond, the prominent clergyman and Yale Chaplain Reverend William Sloane Coffin and the Catholic priest Father Philip Berrigan, who with his brother Daniel were for awhile on the FBI's "Ten Most Wanted" list for their anti-war activism. I also recruited Leonard Weinglass who had represented, among others, the Chicago Seven—Tom Hayden, Yippie Abbie Hoffman and others accused of criminal organizing around the Chicago Convention in '68, civil rights/anti-war radical Angela Davis, and the actress/anti-war advocate Jane Fonda. So from the very beginning, we let the government know we were going to mount an aggressive, dramatic defense.

Then, of course, there were two other components for an effective defense that I had to put together. One was an organizing effort to get sympathetic supporters from across the country to create and maintain interest in the Ellsberg trial as an important anti-war activity. And then there was the reality that an effort like we were planning was going to cost a lot of money, so I took it upon myself to raise a lot of money.

When the decision was made to hold the trial in Los Angeles because the actual documents were copied at a small advertising agency in Los Angeles, I approached Betty with the idea that we had to go back to California, not to Santa Barbara, but to LA We would have to live there so I could be on top of the organizing and fundraising as well as being present at the trial once it got underway. I believe that in her heart, Betty wasn't all that wild about returning to the city where she was raised. She had a number of unpleasant memories and a number of good ones, but Betty saw the logic of my arguments and she was completely committed to the cause of getting Ellsberg a fair trial. So, we packed up everything and moved again back to the West Coast.

I set up two offices on 4th Street in downtown Los Angeles. One office was a non-profit organization to raise money for the trial, and another was a political organization to publicize the issues and coordinate our efforts with other anti-war activists around the country. Believe me, in some ways, raising money was the easy part because riding herd on all the disparate anti-war groups who had agendas around the Pentagon Papers was a hair-pulling, nerve-racking adventure. There was even one militant wing that insisted Ellsberg should be tried as a war criminal for his activities at the Defense Department before he released the papers. To say the least, that did not seem to me like a particularly brilliant idea.

So, as I put my various plans into action, I often reminded myself to let all the different elements and people "juggle themselves." And it worked beyond my wildest expectations. Over the next year, I was destined to become involved with many powerful and influential people who would be allies in crucial national and international conflicts. And I owe my confidence that I could be successful working that way to the insights provided me by my good friend and confidant Arthur Krim.

CHAPTER EIGHT
Hooray For Hollywood

Hooray for Hollywood, that screwy ballyhooey Hollywood. "Hooray For Hollywood," music and lyrics by Johnny Mercer/Richard Whiting, 1937.

When I first became involved with the Daniel Ellsberg trial and the *Pentagon Papers*, I was very upbeat, looking forward to the recognition I hoped to receive from my old friends and my family, especially my mother who still dismissed everything I accomplished as "a waste of time." She continued to ask when I would get a "real job" like my older brother who was a *shmata* salesman and my younger brother who worked for the State Department. Needless to say, her needling did little for my self-esteem, but my old New York friends, and new friends like Arthur Krim provided a solid base for me to begin my efforts to support Ellsberg.

Then, when the trial was moved to Los Angeles, I had a new problem because I needed to raise a lot of money and I didn't really know that many people with money in Los Angeles to help me get our efforts off the ground. At that time, the connection between Santa Barbara and LA was not so strong. My best friend, the writer Bob Scheer who had also moved to Los Angeles, was certainly not close to the money interests given his left-leaning politics. There were not, and still aren't, many major corporations headquartered in LA I knew there was a lot of California old money centered around Pasadena, but it tended to be held by a very conservative group which wasn't, to say the least, a friend of progressive causes. That left Hollywood as my potential primary funding source. And, to quote the hoary tale told about the famous outlaw Willie Sutton who answered, when asked why he robbed banks, "…'Cause that's where the money is," I began to work the Hollywood crowd because that's where the money was. And okay, it's true, sure, it didn't hurt that I was married to Betty Warner.

Most people now assume that Hollywood producers, directors and actors have always been big contributors to political causes, especially liberal causes, but that's not correct. Of course, everyone has heard about writers who were blacklisted, accused of being communists during the (Joe) McCarthy era. Unfortunately, there weren't huge fundraisers to support them.

It's true that the Hollywood community was (and is) sort of genially Democratic, but in the early '70s, their political activism had not yet been organized into the kind of effective fund raising Krim had been involved with in New York. The somewhat derogatory appellation "radical chic" developed from the glitzy, arty, liberal fundraising parties in New York, not in Los Angeles.

Well, I'm not going to claim I am solely responsible for creating the archetypal left-liberal fundraising apparatus in Hollywood which has become so infamous to Republicans and a generous source of much needed cash for progressives, but since I'm setting these things down near the end of my life in order to have the guilty pleasure of believing my story will garner some of the recognition I gave up when I was working behind the scenes, yes, I was instrumental, absolutely instrumental in creating that fundraising juggernaut. Our group included, at times, such major stars as Paul Newman, Barbra Streisand, Robert Redford, Burt Lancaster, Neil Diamond and Warren Beatty, the hugely successful producers Norman Lear and Sydney Pollack, along with business people like Harold Willens, co-founder of Business Executives Move For Peace In Vietnam; Ted Ashley, chairman of Warner Bros.; Attorney/Businessman Miles L. Rubin, an original founder of Energy Action; and entrepreneurial investors like Leo Wyler and Max Palevsky. Some of these people were also central figures in our fundraising group that came to be known as the "Malibu Mafia," but I made my first contact with most of them managing the fundraising for Daniel Ellsberg.

Believe me, I am not taking anything away from Ellsberg himself. He was (and is) a courageous, charismatic figure, every bit the hero he was made out to be, and his personality was a huge asset when it came to raising money. He was also absolutely essential in organizing the strategy for his own defense, and he was very good at it. His only weakness was, like certain other intense, highly intelligent people, he tended to focus on the details and often missed the bigger picture. For example, one day he was terribly curious about how the Kennedy/Johnson administrations made deals with notorious Vietnamese autocrats like President Ngo Dinh Diem or the prime minister in the military junta, Nguyen Cao Ky. One afternoon, when Ellsberg insisted on having yet another meeting after we'd been in court all morning, I remember him asking me something like, "Sheinbaum, who was the CIA agent who dealt directly with Ky?"

"I don't know," I said, "that was after I left the Michigan State project."

Ellsberg turned to one of his lawyers, either Boudin or Weinglass. "We have to know the name of that contact person!"

The lawyer, I think it was Boudin, just shrugged. He obviously had other things on his mind. Ellsberg turned back to me. "We need to get someone on this Sheinbaum."

I was annoyed. "Why? We have all our people out organizing across the country to make the public aware of your trial. You and your trial are some of the most important, if not *the* most important anti-war symbols right now. Who cares who was the CIA agent who dealt directly with Nguyen Cao Ky."

Ellsberg was agitated. "You don't get it do you, Sheinbaum? You just don't get it."

"Get what?"

It was at that point in the conversation, when Boudin excused himself. "I don't have time for this. I have to get ready for court tomorrow. You two can discuss ancient history."

Ellsberg was left to debate with me. "We have to know everything, Stanley. Absolutely everything. We've got to document it, get it into the record."

Well, I didn't have time for those discussions either, so to placate Ellsberg I told him we'd research the question, but I had no intention of using one of our volunteers to do that. The next day would only bring new questions about other minute details and I was definitely determined to focus on the big picture.

In fact, my organizing and fundraising efforts often made it impossible for me to spend as much time in the courtroom as I would have liked. I remember there was a payphone just outside the court. For those of you who are too young to know, a payphone was a land line that you could use to make a call after depositing a certain amount of change in little slots on the top of the machine. Well every day I arrived at the courthouse with a huge bag of quarters, and I spent much of my time on that damn payphone working with our organizers around the country and calling people to try and raise money. Obviously, I was finding that being a behind-the-scenes guy and an effective go-between often isn't so very glamorous. Not very glamorous at all—walking around with bags of quarters that weighed down my pockets and made my jackets lopsided.

It turned out that Ellsberg's wife, Patricia, Pat, was also terrific at meeting people and very persuasive talking to groups about her husband and the trial. Interestingly enough, her father, Louis Marx, was an enormously rich industrialist, an American toymaker known as the "*Toy*coon" of the toy business He was very right-wing in his politics, very close to Richard Nixon, and he considered Ellsberg a traitor to his country. Patricia, however, was warm and enthusiastic and very human in her presentations, which made her an effective emissary on trips to places like Omaha or Phoenix or Columbus. Daniel was lucky to have her on his team. So were we, although it goes without saying that her family never donated any money to the cause.

One of my constant conflicts was to walk that thin line between the need to inspire confidence in our "troops," and yet not give the impression we were likely to win at trial. Paradoxically, unlike a political race where success only breeds more success, it's hard to raise money for a cause if the cause appears already successful. At first, the fact that Ellsberg was even arrested was enough of a shock to bring in donations. Then, when the government actually decided to prosecute and charge him under the Espionage Act of 1917, plus other charges including theft and conspiracy which together carried a total maximum sentence of 115 years, the flow of donations increased dramatically. However, as the pre-trial period dragged on, we were constantly in danger of disappearing from public view and the donations slowed to a trickle. That's why we needed a political organization as well as a fundraising organization—to help maintain public interest.

The political people, mostly young volunteers, many of them students, were by and large very effective in maintaining our notoriety on college campuses, in churches and among liberal political organizations. We could not have been successful without them. But there were also militants like those who wanted to put Ellsberg himself on trial because they said he was a war criminal before he became an anti-war hero. Such ideological purity was obviously a problem despite the tenacious energy and dedication on antiwar issues the militants held.

The trial also occurred during the time when the somewhat extreme version of "participatory democracy," which had evolved from the Berkeley Free Speech Movement, was in vogue among political activists. This version required that all the different individuals who had an interest in a particular situation should also have the right to participate in the decisions involving that situation. In our case, it meant that the more militant supporters also wanted a say in what strategy the lawyers should follow. Even though Boudin and Weinglass were very left-liberal lawyers who had represented some of the most radical defendants in America, it was inconceivable for me to imagine them working under the direction of a committee of students no matter how well-intentioned.

At first I tried to mollify the militants by telling them we would pass on their ideas to the lawyers. But they would have none of that. One of the more aggressive activists confronted me with a demand that she be "in the room with Ellsberg and the lawyers to determine how to best destroy fortress Amerika." She emphasized the "k" as was the style at that time.

"The lawyers won't have it," I objected.

"Then fire those pig lawyers," she said.

I had to smile. "Boudin and Weinglass, pig lawyers? You want to ask Angela Davis or Abbie Hoffman about that?"

"That was then, this is now. We want a vote about trial strategy!"

Finally, I'd had it. "Look," I said, "I've got a big job to do and I'm going to do it. Either you support us our way or just get out of the way. It's that simple."

She was furious. "You're an old jerk, Stanley K. Sheinbaum, and an asshole too, a traitor to the movement. You'll get yours, you government fink!" She stormed out of the office.

Maybe I was an old jerk to her, after all, I was in my early fifties at the time, but a fink? I don't know where she came up with that unless she assumed that because I was working with a lot of rich, successful people, I must be somehow connected to the government. I suppose that's not a wholly irrational assumption, given what we've learned about the sorts of people really big money supports.

Out biggest fundraiser was an event that has gone down in the history of fantastic liberal fundraising events. On April 7, 1973, on Daniel Ellsberg's 42nd birthday, we held a huge gala at the mansion of a top talent agent turned movie producer, Jennings Lang. Everyone who walked through his door paid significant money just to be there including the celebrities, among them, Joni Mitchell, David Geffen,

Ringo Starr, John Lennon and George Harrison, Yoko Ono, and the agent Freddie Fields. Peter Bogdanovich, Diahann Carroll, Hugh Hefner, Burt Lancaster, and Sally Kellerman also attended. But the big attraction, the reason the event was so successful, was that Barbra Streisand performed throughout the evening accompanied by the incomparable Marvin Hamlisch on piano.

Barbra was extraordinary. First of all, she looked incredibly beautiful in a beige, low-cut silk gown. Her hair was piled on top of her head and held there with some sort of clip that looked to be made of diamonds that sparkled like her eyes as she sang song after song. And the agreement was that each song would be requested by a member of the audience willing to pay really big bucks to hear her sing it live. She sang dozens of songs, but some of the more memorable moments were a version of "I'll Get By" dedicated to Ellsberg but paid for by Lang, "I Don't Know where I Stand" for the producer David Geffen and, believe it or not, "Twinkle, Twinkle Little Star" for writer/comedian, Carl Reiner. We raised more than $50,000.00, a significant sum even in today's dollars.

Although Barbra later sang at a George McGovern fundraiser I organized, I remember that night at Jennings Lang's mansion with a great deal of nostalgia and a certain bittersweet sadness when I realize that I will not experience such an evening again.

Thinking about Barbra at the McGovern fundraiser reminds me that while the Ellsberg trial was in hiatus in 1972, George McGovern became the Democratic nominee for president of the United States, and I was his chief fundraiser in Southern California. Unfortunately, McGovern is often remembered primarily for one of the Democratic Party's most depressing electoral disasters—he suffered an overwhelming defeat to Nixon with Electoral College totals of 520 to 17. McGovern carried only Massachusetts and Washington, D.C. He even failed to win his home state of South Dakota, but he was popular with the Hollywood crowd and around Southern California in general so it was relatively easy to raise money for his campaign.

I've always felt McGovern should have been more popular nationally. He was a bright, kind, moral, decorated veteran of World War II, a highly respected US Senator, a really decent, good man who ran at a time when the stars were aligned against him, as I sometimes fear the stars always are for bright, kind, moral, decent men and women. Well, of course, not only the stars, but also the Watergate "plumbers"—those crooks and dirty tricksters and out-and-out evil manipulators from the Nixon campaign who were also behind the break-ins at Ellsberg's psychiatrist's office.

In the end, our newly formed fundraising group did come through for McGovern. We raised tons of money on behalf of the national campaign, and gained the respect of numerous Democrats around the country including future president Bill Clinton and First Lady, Senator and Secretary of State Hillary Clinton. At that time, the Clintons were running the McGovern campaign in Texas. I did feel truly sad about how poorly McGovern did in the election, but I also felt really good about my hard work for him. I suppose I can honestly say I was again reminded that not all losses are defeats. If nothing else, that lopsided election was soon followed by Nixon's complete humiliation and resignation.

Meanwhile, at the Ellsberg trial, things were happening behind the scenes that were to determine the eventual outcome even more than the proceedings taking place in open court. When people sometimes question why top lawyers are paid so well, they fail to understand that a case is often determined by the hard work the lawyers and their support teams perform outside the courtroom. The Ellsberg case deftly illustrates what I mean. Our lawyers discovered that the government prosecutors were withholding the evidence that connected that break-in at the office of Daniel Ellsberg's psychiatrist, Lewis Fielding, to the Watergate scandal. It turned out that the Nixon/Erlichman/Liddy controlled group that broke into the Democratic offices at the Watergate Hotel—the scandal that eventually brought down Nixon—were the very same crooks working for Liddy who had previously broken into Fielding's office to try and find dirt on Ellsberg. When the trial judge, William Matthew Byrne, Jr., ordered the prosecution to hand that information over to our defense team, the government's case began to crumble.

Then came revelations about Judge Byrne himself. I had occasion to meet with Judge Byrne in his chambers, and I must say I really liked the guy. We also, after the trial ended, ran into each other numerous times at different events in LA, and I would even say we were casual friends up until his death a few years ago. I thought his rulings during the trial were fair and straightforward, but his life story, one in which he was seriously mentioned as a future nominee to the Supreme Court, became instead another tragic tale triggered by the corruption and deceit of the Nixon administration.

I remember the day Leonard Boudin pulled me aside and in a hushed but excited voice told me their discovery requests had pried loose new information about Byrne.

I asked Boudin, "What kind of information?"

"You're not gonna' believe this, Stanley." He was smiling, an expression not commonly seen on Leonard Boudin's face during trial.

"What…so what is it I'm not going to believe?"

"Guess?"

"Oh, come on, Boudin."

"Okay. Turns out Nixon's chief hatchet man John Erlichman, after the trial had already started, called Byrne into his White House office and offered Byrne a job as head of the F.B.I. once the trial was over."

"Did Byrne accept the offer?"

"Doesn't matter," said Boudin gleefully. "The offer in itself contaminates the trial."

Well, my sympathetic view of Judge Byrne turned out to be accurate because he didn't try to hide his conversation with Erlichman once it became known to us. He even revealed his contact with Erlichman in open court, and then a few days later, on May 11th, 1973, Judge Byrne declared a mistrial. Bye-bye Byrne's chance for a Supreme Court appointment, but hello the end to Daniel Ellsberg's legal troubles. We won against what had seemed, just a few years earlier, to be insurmountable odds. In the process, we had raised the public's consciousness about the war and how our government controlled access to information. We were, to say the least, jubilant.

Of course, Daniel Ellsberg's victory resulted in a personal victory as well. My standing in the community as an effective go-between and behind the scenes fundraiser rose astronomically, and I was quietly known as the go-to-guy for liberal fundraising in the LA area. Betty and I started opening our house up for political and cultural salons organized around causes we cared about. Things were really going well, and I felt like my new life had been my destiny all along, and that I had, more or less, arrived.

However, I wasn't satisfied to rest on my accomplishments. After all, I was still that struggling Stanley K. Sheinbaum inside my head, needing to prove myself against greater and greater challenges, and I was momentarily perplexed as to where I should next direct my energies. It was clear that US involvement in Vietnam was coming to an end although we had no idea it would be such an ignominious end— the panicked evacuation of the American embassy in Saigon while desperate refugees scrambled to get onto helicopters on the roof of the compound and the complete collapse of the South Vietnamese army. It was such a terrible ending to such a sad humiliating time. But the struggle really was over, and it was time for me to look in new directions.

I had been thinking a great deal about the fact that I'd spent all those years training to be an economist, and it was actually economic issues more than international affairs that captured my deepest concern. In a sense, my involvement with Vietnam, Papandreou and then Vietnam again had all happened by accident. I was caught up in those times, saw a need to act and was uniquely positioned to act, so I did. Proudly and effectively. Yet, when I looked at the issues that were troubling me most about my country, I could see clearly, as an economist, that they were economic issues: the growing disparity between rich and poor, the dominance of corporate wealth and power, the degradation of our environment through greed and neglect. However, it is one thing to see these problems, and quite another to figure out effective ways to attack them.

As I deliberated what to do, I turned again to my best friend and most honest critic, Betty. She said, "Why don't you go back to teaching, Stanley? You were a wonderful teacher, your students loved you and you could be such an inspiration to the next generation."

I told her I'd thought about teaching, but the idea didn't excite me the way it used to.

Betty considered my feelings about teaching. "Well," she said, "of course teaching doesn't excite you. I know you, Stanley, you like to be where the action is. I like that about you. It's wonderful to be around you when you've taken on another project, but I still think you'd make a great teacher."

"I don't know, Betty, maybe you're right. Maybe I should teach. I'm not getting any younger, and I'm tired a lot of the time."

Betty's attitude changed abruptly. "Oh no you don't, Stanley! Don't start acting old and complaining about being tired. You're not even sixty and I've noticed you only complain about being tired when you don't have some new adventure planned. I take back everything I said. If teaching is going to make you old and tired, forget it. Go find some new project that gets you excited."

Well, there actually was one task that had been incubating at the back of my brain. When I was rounding up support for the Ellsberg trial, I had become involved with the ACLU, the American Civil Liberties Union, in order to get their support. They of course jumped on board the Ellsberg defense immediately and were very helpful providing legal assistance. But I also found the Los Angeles chapter to be somewhat moribund, lacking in leadership and conflicted about what direction their efforts should take.

While it's obvious that the ACLU is a great organization that has been, as the literature says, "our nation's guardian of liberty, working daily in courts, legislatures and communities to defend and preserve the individual rights and liberties…" it had, at that time, a very narrow focus. It's true that, prior to it's founding in 1920, the year I was born by the way, many of our civil rights, although enshrined in the American Constitution, were not recognized in the daily lives of most Americans. The ACLU changed that. Still, I felt the question needed to be asked, should civil rights be confined to freedom of speech, religion and assembly? And furthermore, do we not have an obligation, at least if those First Amendment rights are to mean anything, to also fight for the right to have a decent living, a fair wage, adequate health care and a clean environment? Well, as I was to discover, many in the ACLU agreed with me, but there were a significant number of others who did not.

The fight to reinvigorate the ACLU with a wider focus on what constitutes rights and liberties was an intense battle that continues to this day; but it was a struggle I thought worth fighting, and I found an ally in the most amazing woman, Ramona Ripston, who would become the executive director of the LA chapter of the ACLU for almost forty years. In the process, Ramona and Norman Lear, the extraordinarily successful TV producer of a string of hits starting with *All In The Family*, and I, as well as the many, many other supporters who believed in the changes, completely rejuvenated the organization into a powerful force for social change in Southern California and the nation. We certainly became number one enemies of the right who loved to accuse politicians and other public figures of being "card-carrying members of the ACLU," a rather underhanded reference to the political battles of the 1950s when enemies of the right, were accused of being "card-carrying members of the Communist Party." But our notoriety did not come without a struggle.

CHAPTER NINE
Brother Can You Spare A Dime?

"They used to tell me I was building a dream, with peace and glory ahead. Why should I be standing in line, just waiting for bread? "Brother, Can You Spare a Dime," lyrics by Yip Harburg, music by Jay Gorney , 1931.

For an economist, or maybe I should say, for anyone who focuses on economics, questions of civil liberties tend to be framed within the context of money—who has it, who doesn't, who controls it, who creates it. It's all about money, whether one is right, left, or dead center. To most economists it seems perfectly obvious that individual rights are meaningless if they do not include economic rights. That's why Marx was so important. Whether one buys the rest of his economic prescription or not, his theories intrinsically tied human rights to economic rights.

So, in the popular imagination, to the degree that people discuss these issues at all, questions of economic rights have been associated with left-wing politics in the 20th century unless one was a fanatic reader of Ayn Rand. In fact, economic rights have always been part of the right's agenda as well. Consider the one simple fact that for much of the 18th, 19th, and even 20th centuries, voting rights in so-called democratic nations were usually confined to those who owned property.

Issues about economic rights as essential to any serious discussion of civil liberties were among the topics bandied about in conversations Betty and I had with Ramona Ripston and her husband, federal Appeals Court Judge Stephen Reinhardt. We were staring down at the Mediterranean, sparkling in the sunshine of lazy pine-scented afternoons at the summer home Betty and I owned on Giglio, a small island off the coast of Tuscany. Ramona had recently become the executive director of the ACLU's Los Angeles chapter, the first woman to be chosen as an executive director of any ACLU affiliate in the United States, and she was very intent on persuading me to help her reinvigorate the chapter.

It would be easy to dismiss those discussions as idle philosophizing by successful people who had few economic problems of their own, and there would be an element of truth in that assertion. But, ironically enough, it was absolutely true that economic concerns were at the very heart of whether the LA affiliate would be able to effectively pursue its First Amendment agenda (primarily free speech issues), to say nothing of broader issues of economic inequality, income disparity, and the minimum wage. As Ramona, in her charming but somewhat exasperated manner declared as she leaned across the table on our veranda, "How can I possibly take on broader human rights issues, economic issues I believe are important, if I don't even have the money to hire staff lawyers?"

"What do you mean?"

"Stanley," she said her voice rising a little, "we only have contract lawyers. I don't have any staff lawyers. Not one." Then she settled back into her chair. She smiled and shook her head. "Our office is in this crummy little building on 5th Street in downtown LA…" she started to laugh, "above a greasy spoon coffee shop and a wig store." She did have a delightful laugh. "And, Stanley, and…" she paused for dramatic effect, "need I remind you that we're half a million dollars in debt. That's the ACLU in LA right now. We have our own practical economic issues to deal with before we can think about expanding our mission."

How could I refuse her? "Okay, Ramona. What do you want me to do?"

She laughed again. "I've heard you work miracles, Stanley. Everything. I want you to solve all our problems."

"This Jew doesn't do miracles," I said. "But what about if I set up a non-profit foundation with my friend Norman Lear, and we raise some serious money?" I knew Norman would help since he was a long-time, enthusiastic supporter of the ACLU.

This time her smile reminded me of a very happy little girl, although knowing Ramona she might not like to be described that way. "That would do, Stanley. That would do very well indeed, thank you."

So Norman Lear and I set up a 501c3 non-profit corporation and we began raising money. There were numerous events at the house where Betty and I lived at the time, and things were going very well with the Hollywood crowd that was traditionally sympathetic to issues concerning free speech. I was pleased with our progress, as was Norman. Ramona was thrilled. She hired her first staff lawyer, the brilliant young Mark Rosenbaum, who had recently graduated from Harvard Law, and she began to pay down the chapter's debt. Then the Nazis marched on Skokie.

What did the LA chapter of the ACLU have to do with Nazis in Skokie? Well, in the mid-1970s, Skokie, Illinois, was a small, middle-class, family-oriented suburb northwest of Chicago, known to be heavily Jewish, and many of the village's Jewish families had extended family members who had been imprisoned and were murdered in the concentration camps during the Holocaust.

Now a man by the name of Frank Collin was the head of a very small band of white supremacists who called themselves the National Socialist Party of America (American Nazis). The group was not especially important, a bunch of idiots actually, but Collin was something of a perverse PR genius at calling attention to his motley crew. One of his more brilliantly demented schemes was to apply for a permit to hold a rally in a Skokie park.

When the City of Skokie cleverly agreed to give him the permit if Collin could put up an impossibly huge insurance liability bond, Collin shifted plans and called for a street march on Skokie city hall. Skokie then filed for an injunction to prohibit the march which was granted by the Cook County Circuit Court. As the case wound through the various appeals courts, Collin, Skokie and the militant Jewish Defense League each appealed whichever court decisions didn't go their way, and each time the case received enormous press attention.

Well, this entire brouhaha became an issue for the ACLU of Southern California when the Illinois ACLU entered the dispute and agreed to represent Collin and his Nazis. Of course, the Illinois ACLU's decision made perfect sense within the context of the First Amendment's guarantees of freedom of speech, guarantees that the ACLU was founded to defend and protect. On the other hand, the ACLU's decision rightfully pissed off most American Jews who on that particular issue weren't overly concerned with First Amendment rights, and as a result, many wealthy Jews withheld or withdrew financial support to the ACLU.

I remember one prominent Westside liberal, a very cultured man, who had been a very generous donor to liberal causes. He was livid when I approached him about a donation to the ACLU. All his civility melted away as he hissed at me, "I wouldn't give you bastards a nickel."

"You've helped us in the past…"

"In those days, you weren't defending the men who murdered my family. How could you, Sheinbaum? Have you lost your mind?"

"Look," I said, "Frank Collin hasn't murdered anybody. He hasn't conspired to destroy Jewish property. He hasn't even done anything illegal. Of course you hate him. I hate him. We all hate him, but if we are honest, we hate him because of the things he says, not what he's done. If we really believe in free speech, we have to defend his right to speak freely, no matter how odious his message."

"I don't agree, Stanley. No one has the right to spew venom against our people. We've suffered so much, too much, really."

"Well, then you only believe in free speech if the message is one you want to hear?"

"Cut the crap, Sheinbaum. I don't have to support hate speech and I don't have to listen to your little self-righteous speech either. By the way, don't call me again, understood?"

"About the ACLU?"

"About anything."

You know, when I raise money I get all kinds of refusals and I have to accept all kinds of attitudes, but I had to admit that reactions from Jews angered by the ACLU's defense of the Nazis' right to march in Skokie, were as painful as any I'd ever heard until years later when I was to become involved in the Middle East peace process. The accusations hurt. They really did.

I remember one evening during the Skokie turmoil when I was with Norman Lear going over our strategy to keep funds rolling in despite the hostility and doubt. Norman, who completely and utterly identifies with being Jewish as well as being a much-decorated bomber gunner on B-17s during World War II, was adamant that the best protection for Jews, or for any minority as well, was to have a society where no one could be prosecuted for expressing their thoughts, ideas, or faith.

"Yeah, but I don't know," I said, "if it's smart for us to get into the position of defending Nazis who will cause unbearable pain to the Jews of Skokie."

"That's why I'm involved with the ACLU," said Norman. "We actually stand by what we say we believe in. Free speech. We're committed to it even when it's uncomfortable." He laughed. "You know, Stanley, once those loudmouths march in Skokie, if they march, people will finally see what a rag-tag bunch of slobs they are. And then it will be over for them. Then the media attention will fade away." And Norman was right. That's exactly what happened.

Actually, over the long haul, I believe the ACLU came out of that Skokie battle better off than they were before the turmoil started. The majority of people who care about our freedoms admired the ACLU for the courage to stand up and fight for the principles the organization was founded to protect when it would have been so much easier, and also in the organization's short-term financial interest, to do nothing. In fact, I would have to say a majority of our Hollywood supporters hung in there with us and some even increased their contributions. I suppose that's because actors and directors and writers and producers like Norman Lear are acutely aware of the dangers of censorship. They are, after all, constantly pressured to alter their work to accommodate prevailing public opinion.

Meanwhile the ACLU in LA, under Ramona's leadership and our new foundation's greater financial support, was able to become more active in its struggle to protect our civil liberties. But that success and freedom generated another intense struggle, this time within the organization, about the appropriate ways to broaden the mission and raise our profile. I spent many hours talking to members and persuading them that it would be good for the ACLU if we could also focus on the economic issues that were becoming more important in American society as the gap between rich and poor continued to grow, and the middle class was shrinking. Ramona was equally committed to economic issues, possibly even more than I was, but there were many members and supporters who felt the ACLU should stick to its narrow founding purpose.

The focus of this debate became the Federal Election Campaign Act (FECA) of 1972, which was amended in 1974. FECA placed certain limits on campaign contributions and set up a federal monitoring system. Almost immediately, individuals and groups from both the left and the right began to argue that the restrictions in FECA were unconstitutional because they limited free speech. In other words, in its simplest form, their argument was that the money raised and spent on political campaigns was a form of "speech," and therefore that any restrictions on that money amounted to restricting speech. Then, in the 1976 decision, *Buckley v. Valeo*, the United States Supreme Court more or less agreed that restrictions on money were restrictions on speech. Many in the ACLU, including the National ACLU, agreed with the Supreme Court's decision.

I was furious. I met with Ramona and let out all my frustration. "How can we possibly argue we're protecting civil liberties if we allow big money to control the election process? 'Money is speech'. What absolute nonsense. The little guy won't have a chance. Civil liberties will become meaningless."

"I agree with you, Stanley."

"What is the ACLU thinking?"

"I agree, Stanley."

"Is this organization being run by right-wing Republicans?"

"Are you listening? I said, I agree with you, Stanley."

"Oh yeah…. Sorry." I felt a little foolish because I knew she opposed the decision as much as I did. "So, what should we do?"

"Well, there's not too much we can do other than make our arguments to national and hope they adopt our point of view in the future. And our LA affiliate doesn't have to take the same position that the national organization has. We can come out against *Buckley v. Valeo,* but I'm sure as hell not going to use scarce LA money to protest the decision. The Supreme Court has decided. There are many, many other economic battles I want to litigate, Stanley. Important battles."

Well, ACLU in LA did come out in favor of campaign finance reform and we did consistently argue that equating campaign donations with speech has further corrupted the already corrupt campaign financing of US elections. But we were fighting a losing battle.

In fact, as I reflect back on that decision, we may have not only lost that battle but also the war. Recently, a Supreme Court decision established that since corporations are legally "persons," there can be no restrictions on their campaign donations. This seems completely absurd to me, but more than the absurdity of the ruling, such a decision means, in practical terms, that American politics will increasingly become the playground of large corporations and extremely rich individuals. This will totally undermine any pretensions about democracy in American politics.

But if we were losing the election law battles, we were winning on other fronts. Ramona really was committed to expanding the practice of civil liberties law to include litigating for economic justice, and boy, did we get into some great tussles with powerful interests.

At one point, Ramona came to the board and asked for our support in filing a suit against the State of California to maintain at least minimum standards in all of the public schools. This was after numerous fact-finding missions found many of the state's poorest schools in absolutely deplorable condition, paint peeling, nonfunctioning bathrooms, broken windows, dangerous playgrounds, no books, no functioning communications equipment, unqualified teachers. After we filed suit, the State of California, under a Democratic governor no less, Gray Davis, unbelievably, fought back and set aside 14 million to fight the ACLU. Ramona didn't back down and we finally won that battle when the new *Republican* Governor Arnold Schwarzenegger settled the case, Williams v. California, much to the chagrin of many of his supporters.

Then, when the infamous Proposition 187, the California initiative passed by voters denied public services to undocumented immigrants, Ramona came to the board and said the ACLU in Los Angeles was going to help block 187. Certain board members questioned whether we should join the lawsuits. "This isn't our fight," they argued. "The people of California voted for the proposition, let others carry the ball on this one." I could tell Ramona was getting pissed, so I jumped in. "This is ridiculous. 187 will, in effect, force principals to expel immigrant children from our public schools. How can we possibly say we believe in civil liberties if we're going to throw poor immigrant kids out of our schools?" Arguments went back and forth, but those of us urging the organization to get involved won the argument, and ACLU in Los Angeles joined in the lawsuits against Proposition 187, which was ruled unconstitutional by a federal judge, whose decision was not appealed.

More recently, we won a ruling from the federal court that stopped the LAPD from arresting homeless people for sitting, lying or sleeping on public streets. Again we argued that people were losing their liberty primarily for economic reasons—because they were poor and had no place to live. The court agreed.

We supported the janitors union when its members struck the hotels in order to get a living wage. Again, the basic issue was that these poor workers were not being paid enough to support themselves and their families. As a result, they were in effect without liberty to enjoy the other rights they presumably had. We argued that obviously their poverty had a detrimental effect on their freedom. The legal outcome has yet to be determined, but the strike itself was partially successful.

All through those years, we continued to have passionate disagreements with the national ACLU. For example, when President Bush *pere* nominated Clarence Thomas to serve on the Supreme Court, national backed the nomination. No, that's not exactly fair. Technically, they refused to oppose him, which in that charged and extremely controversial situation amounted to support. I remember calling

Ramona to ask her once again, "What's going on with the national ACLU?"

"They just don't get it," she fumed. "They say he will succeed in being appointed to the court anyway, and the lawyers at national prefer not to argue before a justice they publicly opposed."

"But we broke that long standing position not to oppose nominees back in 1987, when we opposed Robert Bork. Thomas has to be worse than Bork. Did they listen to the Anita Hill's testimony about his pornographic references in the workplace? Have they reviewed his incredible, so called "originalist" judicial opinions which would remove decades of precedent on civil liberties issues? Have they even noticed that the NAACP, the Urban League, and the National Organization for Women oppose the appointment?" I was really getting myself worked up.

"Well, again, Stanley, we don't have to go along. We can oppose the Thomas nomination." And so we did, much to the annoyance of the national board.

But the most passionate struggles and the greatest impact that Ramona, Mark Rosenbaum, and I have had was on Los Angeles itself, primarily in our dealings with the Los Angeles Police Department—the LAPD.

The LAPD was hated and feared for many years because of known incidents of corruption and officers' use of excessive force, especially against minorities. There were also allegations of illegal spying, usually against leftist political groups but also against, among others, the National Council of Churches, the Unitarian Church, the National Organization for Women (NOW), the Gay Liberation Front and even the state-funded Educational Opportunity Program. Dangerous people, right? Well, that's the way things were until Ramona and the ACLU began to initiate and/or support a number of lawsuits against the police department.

During that period when the ACLU was pushing to reform the LAPD, I learned a great deal about the internal workings of the department. Then, in the early '90s, when it became increasingly apparent that some action needed to be taken to push reform, Mayor Tom Bradley, an African-American and an ex-police officer himself, appointed me to the Los Angeles Police Commission. Then, through an unlikely series of coincidences, I became the president of the Police Commission. Well, that raised a ruckus—one of the board members of the ACLU was the president of the Police Commission! Ramona and I had more than a few chuckles about that.

The times were, however, not humorous. The infamous Daryl Gates was police chief, and he was a tough, arrogant cop who built his reputation as a law and order guy willing to come down hard on people he didn't like. I was definitely one of the people he didn't like, but there was little he could do against me, or that I could do against him because on the one hand, the mayor supported me, and on the other, Gates was very popular with the people and the press. So we had between us a sort of détente until the police officers who were behind the Rodney King beating were found not guilty, and the city exploded into an orgy of burning, looting, shooting, and mayhem.

On the day when the troubles broke out, I jumped into my car and despite the danger, headed downtown to police headquarters. Just as I was pulling into the building, I saw Gates leaving. I asked him where he was going.

"It's none of your business, Sheinbaum, but there's a luncheon I have to attend over on the Westside," he said. "I have to put in an appearance, but I'll only stay for two minutes."

"But chief, I said, "don't you know what's going on in the streets?"

Gates just shook his head disdainfully as he got into his car. "Of course I do. I'm the chief. It's nothing we haven't seen before from those people. Anyway, I'll be right back."

Well, I knew the luncheon was in fact a fundraiser. Gates had political aspirations, and I knew a number of the people who were going to be at the luncheon. In fact, I had been invited to attend, but, because I was president of the Police Commission, I thought it would be better if I was not there. Once the streets were in complete chaos, I knew for certain I shouldn't be there. But neither should Gates.

Anyway, Gates stayed much longer than two minutes. He made a speech that ran for at least an hour while the city was falling apart. Meanwhile, I remained downtown huddled with municipal, state, and federal officials including Representative Maxine Waters. Maxine represented a large part of South Los Angeles in Congress, and she was very upset by the events going on in her neighborhoods. Later, she commented that the turmoil was, in her eyes, a rebellion. "If you call it a riot, it sounds like it was just a bunch of crazy people who went out and did bad things for no reason. I maintain it was somewhat understandable, if not acceptable," she said. Anyway, at the time, we were trying to determine how we were going to deal with the turmoil, which had spread from the initial limited area around an intersection in Watts, the southern part of the city, to Hollywood on the north, Culver City on the west, and all the way to downtown, where angry crowds were actually laying siege to Parker Center, the police headquarters, while we were inside.

Of course our focus was on how we could calm things down. The city was eventually brought back together by courageous black leadership and the cooperation of caring whites who were not intimidated by the situation. I remember Maxine and I were called to a city park that was completely surrounded by a police cordon which had enclosed a number of angry black youths inside. It was an ugly situation and had the potential to erupt into serious violence. Maxine said, "I'm going in there, Stanley, and I'm bringing those kids out."

I immediately said, "I'm going with you."

Maxine looked at me. "Stanley, umm, do you think that's a good idea? I mean…"

"You mean do I know I'm an old, white guy?"

Maxine sort of smiled. "Okay then, Stanley, let's go."

We walked on into the park, and I really wasn't afraid although maybe I should have been. The young men were as much frightened as anything else, and they respected the fact that Maxine and I were willing to talk to them. They all knew who Maxine was, but I was surprised when I heard a few of them muttering my name, "It's Sheinbawwwwm, man, you know, that Sheinbawwwwm guy…" which sort of pleased me. I guess they'd seen me on TV taking on Daryl Gates.

Maxine and I were able to convince those kids that if they just walked out of the park with us, nothing would happen to them, although we weren't absolutely positive how the police would react even though we were pretty sure they weren't going to attack the president of the Police Commission and a congresswoman. So we just walked out of that park with these kids around us, but as we left, the police made a few tentative moves in our direction. That was the scariest time for me, but I raised my hand and the police finally backed off.

Maxine and I both let out a sigh of relief. "Thanks, Stanley," she said.

"For what?" I asked.

"For just being there, being here with us. It's good for these kids to see that, you know."

Weeks later, after order was restored, I circulated a memo to the other commissioners detailing Gates' actions on the first day of the riots. Well, needless to say, he wasn't untouchable after that. He had lost his power, and eventually, rather quickly actually, we were able to get rid of him. Unfortunately, not long after Gates resigned, I was also forced out. Many, including me, thought it was a time for healing in the police department and I had become a symbol of the anti-Gates faction that had removed a man many on the force still considered "their chief." But I had accomplished much of what I had hoped to accomplish, so I left without a struggle.

In the years that followed, we were to find that even though things were changing within the LAPD, the problems ran far deeper than just Chief Gates. It is to the credit of the ACLU, to Mark Rosenbaum and Ramona Ripston, among others, that pressure to reform the department continued to be applied until another series of scandals placed the LAPD under a Los Angeles Superior Court Order, Order 40, which mandated court supervised reforms in the department.

My involvement with the ACLU was one of the best things I've ever done, but I also felt a slight sense of irony about my situation. There I was, a Stanford-trained economist and a wealthy man, with a spacious Brentwood house filled with beautiful art and photos of myself with famous people from Hollywood, politics and business, a man who had finally gained much of the respect and recognition from my peers that I had always wanted, a person of consequence in Los Angeles and even nationally, a major fundraiser for all sorts of worthy causes. But I was often feeling more and more alienated from the mainstream as I became painfully aware of the serious economic dislocations we Americans were facing and of the apparent inability of the system to deal with them. At times I felt disoriented, unsure of where I should turn next, of what I should do to help develop solutions for so many problems. I was certain the answer lay in continuing to be involved and committed to change. And I certainly learned that from the persistent determination of Ramona Ripston and the ACLU.

(left) Stanley getting ready to join Santa Barbara campaign parade.

(right) Stanley after he joined Bobby Kennedy in Kennedy's car during the Santa Barbara campaign.

(left) Stanley with United Farm Workers president César Chávez during Sheinbaum's run for Congress.

(left) Stanley signals "V" for victory during campaign appearance with Democratic Presidential primary campaigner Senator Eugene McCarthy, although in the end neither emerged

(right) Stanley and Senator McCarthy enjoy a humorous moment during a campaign fundraiser with Paul Newman. (photo: Peter Borsari)

(left) Stanley expresses his relief to United Auto Workers executive board member Paul Schrade's following Schrade's full recovery from critical head wounds received during the assassination of Bobby Kennedy at the Ambassador Hotel in Los Angeles.

(left, l. to r.) Daniel Ellsberg, Patricia Marx Ellsberg and Stanley outside the courthouse during Ellsberg's Pentagon Papers trial.

(right) Stanley participates in a note-taking session discussing Ellsberg's defense strategy.

(right) John Lennon, Yoko Ono and Ringo Starr chat with Barbra Streisand at the star-studded "GALA" fundraiser where Barbra sang requests to raise money for Ellsberg's defense team. (photo:Peter Borsari)

(left) Stanley, far left, and Andreas Papandreou, far right, meet with Swedish government officials when Papandreou was sent into exile after his release from prison by the Greek military junta which had jailed him and threatened to execute him.

(right) Stanley and Andreas Papandreou during happier times after Papandreou had been elected prime minister of Greece and was visiting the Sheinbaums' in Santa Barbara, California.

(left) Stanley and Margaret "Maggie" Papandreou with her son George, who later was elected prime minister of Greece only to face the intense turmoil surrounding the Euro debt crisis.

(left, l.-r.) Stanley, Colorado Senator Gary Hart, South Dakota Senator George McGovern, Vice President Walter Mondale and Warren Beatty vow to defeat Ronald Reagan in 1984.
(photo: Los Angeles Times)

(right, l.-r.) Stanley and Harvard Professor Richard Parker visit China.

wàn bù yào wàng jì jiē jí dòu zī

万不要忘记阶级斗！

NEVER FORGET CLASS STRUGGLE !

(left) Stanley introduces Senator Gary Hart (over Stanley's right shoulder) during one of the hundreds of "salons" held at the Sheinbaums' house over the years.
(photo: Barry Levine)

(left) Stanley in deep discussion with Congresswoman Maxine Waters during an ACLU fundraiser.

(right) Stanley introduces Gregory Peck to speak at ACLU dinner.
(photo: Michael Jacobs)

(left, l.-r.) Los Angeles Times Associate Editor Narda Zacchino, Betty Sheinbaum, jounalist Robert Scheer and Stanley during ACLU benefit.

(right, l. to r.) Stanley, Los Angeles mayor Tom Bradley and ACLU executive director, Ramona Ripston at the opening of the ACLU's new Los Angeles headquarters.

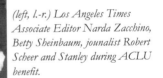

CHAPTER TEN
Paper Doll

She's gone away and left me just like all dolls do. I'll tell you boys…it's tough to love a doll that's not your own. "Paper Doll," music and lyrics by Johnny S. Black, 1915.

While I continued to struggle for ways to apply my increasing awareness of the truly upsetting economic inequality in the United States, I realized I needed to develop influence beyond political fundraising and international negotiations. By the early 1980s, it became obvious to me that one of the reasons the right—conservative economists, conservative Republicans, conservative legislators in general, many of them Democrats—had risen in influence and power is because they have funneled huge amounts of money into various think tanks such as the American Enterprise Institute, the Heritage Foundation, and the Hoover Institution, as well as influential, if small, publications including *The National Review*, *The American Spectator* and *Human Events*. The neo-con, Marty Peretz, even bought *The New Republic*, previously a liberal-left publication, and turned its editorial policy to the right on many issues, especially Israel and the Middle East.

I know think tanks, organizations that conduct research and engage in advocacy about such things as social policy, political strategy, economics, science or technology, and business, or military matters, are not particularly well known to the general public, but the ideas formed in the think tanks are initially disseminated through sympathetic small magazines and newsletters into academia and government. These ideas eventually find their way into our laws and government policies. That's why think tanks are so important.

As conservatives are wont to point out, up until the 1960s and early 1970s, the best known and most influential think tanks were either centrist or somewhat liberal, i.e., the famous Brookings Institution, or the less famous but powerful Center for the Study of Democratic Institutions, where I was a resident scholar in the 1960s. However, as I surveyed the intellectual landscape of the late 1970s and the 1980s I could clearly see that it was the conservative think tanks that were gaining dramatically in power and influence. They certainly had the ear of the Reagan Administration as well as up and coming influential Republican legislators like Newt Gingrich. I felt that if I was going to have influence on the ideas that were setting the agenda for the forthcoming national debates over the economy, I needed to burnish my intellectual and academic credentials because I hadn't been directly involved with the world of ideas since I left the Center in Santa Barbara years ago.

At the time when I was having these thoughts, in the mid-1970s, Jerry Brown was governor of California for his first term, and it occurred to me that since he and I cared about many of the same issues—among them, economic inequality, access to quality education, fair immigration policies—and because of my academic background at Stanford, Michigan State and the Center, I could probably persuade Jerry to appoint me to one of the recently opened positions on the University of California Board of Regents. There was only one little embarrassing problem: I had not originally supported Jerry Brown in his run to become governor. Oh well, I reminded myself that all is fair in love and war and politics, so I decided to contact him anyway.

Over two or three weeks, I was finally able to set up a meeting with Governor Brown, and although he was often in Los Angeles where he had a home, we met at his office in Sacramento, in a fairly formal situation. I assumed we met there to reinforce his status as governor which of course made sense. We discussed a number of important issues concerning the university, primarily that Brown wanted to broaden the make-up of the student body as well as the minority representation on the Board of Regents. We easily agreed on the issue of including greater minority representation in the make-up of the student body at the numerous campuses that comprise the university. I also agreed we should have members on the Board of Regents who more accurately reflect the population of the state, but I did so somewhat sheepishly since I was, after all, obviously an older, white male myself, as were almost all the other regents at that time. In recognition of that fact, I believe I made my pitch based on my liberal viewpoint and attitude being added to a board that was at that juncture, after eight years of Reagan, very conservative.

"Well," said Jerry, "in fact your left-liberal politics may be a problem, Sheinbaum, since you have to be approved by a Republican State Senate."

"I have Republican friends," I countered.

Jerry smiled. "Get serious, Stanley. Your Republican friends are more liberal than many of my Democratic friends."

"Well, yes," I had to agree, "but they also donate money to Republican campaigns. That will carry some weight."

"It will," said the governor, "that's true." He hesitated a moment. "Speaking of campaign contributions, you know, that brings up an interesting issue."

I kept my mouth shut, but I could see it coming.

"I don't believe I saw your name on a list of my supporters during my primary campaign."

"Uhhh…well, Governor Brown, no you couldn't have."

"Why not?"

So he was playing with me. I decided honesty was the best policy. "I supported Joe Alioto because he asked me to, and I committed my support early on."

"Bad choice, Sheinbaum. He's got too many problems from when he was mayor of San Francisco. He supported Hubert Humphrey as well. In '68. At the convention. Not exactly your politics."

"He asked me to help. I told him, yes. I'm loyal."

"Hmmm, well maybe the fact that you didn't contribute in the primary can work in our favor. The press can't say I would be appointing a long-time supporter."

At that point, I knew I had a good chance to get his approval.

When the meeting ended and we shook hands, Jerry, leaned in with that aggressive look he sometimes gets when pressing a point. "That loyalty thing. Don't forget, loyalty *is* important to me too."

Governor Brown did appoint me, and my nomination immediately ran into big problems in the State Senate, just as Jerry said it would. When I called him to ask for help, the governor referred me to his Chief-of-Staff, none other than Gray Davis! Yes, the man who was to become governor himself years later—the governor who would lead the fight against Ramona and me and the ACLU. But I have to give Gray Davis a lot of credit. He knew how to maneuver around and through the legislature, and he was extremely adept at making deals. I honestly don't know exactly how he pulled it off, but my appointment eventually went through and I became a regent of the University of California, one of the greatest educational and research institutions in the world. I believe we had more Nobel Prize winners on our faculty than almost any other American university including Cal Tech, Stanford and Yale.

I was, and still am, so proud to have been a regent, and it did open even more doors and establish my reputation as a person of substance in California, especially in Los Angeles. Being a UC regent does not make one well known, but the title confers great status with those who do know you're on the board.

More important, I was looking forward to getting involved with the university and the faculty. It was the sort of work I had always envisioned myself doing, except...I soon realized I had been very naïve because involvement with faculty and academic issues was not really the work of the UC Board of Regents. Don't get me wrong. I'm not being ungrateful. Being named a regent of the University of California was one of the most prestigious appointments, actually probably the most prestigious appointment, of my life, easily right up there with being named president of the Los Angeles Police Commission. But I have to tell the truth: regents have almost nothing to do with the academic side of the university and very little to do with the actual operations either. Being a regent is very much a political position, and most of the policy decisions we dealt with were political issues concerning the composition of the board, the general disposition of funds allocated by the legislature, setting annual budgetary parameters and tuition costs, as well as lobbying the legislature and private sources for more funds.

On the other hand, my background in economics and the control that the Board of Regents had over the university's investments gave me an opening to push for disinvestment in South Africa, which in those days was still governed by the apartheid government's strict rules on racial separation that denied blacks any meaningful participation in education, politics, or business. This was also the system that kept Nelson Mandela in prison.

To further set the stage, we tend to forget that Ronald Reagan, both as governor and later as president, staunchly backed the South African status quo. Since I had joined a Board of Regents largely appointed by Reagan, the issue of disinvestment of the university's funds in any South African assets was highly emotionally charged. The Reagan appointees fiercely resisted any movement to disinvest by following that old conservative line that our fiduciary responsibility was to make the "best" investment available and not be swayed by political or moral considerations. I once asked one of the Reagan appointees, who shall remain nameless, if that meant we should have invested in Germany in the '30s as long as the Nazis delivered high rates of interest. He considered that idea for a few moments, and then said, "Yes, I believe we are obligated to have our money earn the highest return we can get."

I was flabbergasted. "Well, what the hell, then let's just give our money to the mafia and let them handle our finances."

He frowned. "Don't be absurd, Sheinbaum," he huffed and walked away from our discussion.

Disinvestment was definitely the right issue at the right time. Universities and governments all over the world were withdrawing support from the doomed South African regime, and public support for disinvestment was overwhelming. Still, many on the board resisted the change, and it took all my negotiating powers of persuasion to move the board toward at least partial disinvestment. In the process, the progressive forces gained power, the conservatives lost power and the Board of Regents began a slow evolution toward more open attitudes. We initiated the policy of having students on the board and also encouraged greater diversity in University of California admissions policies. Those advances alone were worth all the effort I put into them.

So, being a regent really was very important. The work was involving and challenging when we could deal with controversial issues, and my experience and knowledge of economics and fundraising was a valuable asset to the board, but I seldom felt I was involved in the world of ideas. Well, frankly, almost never. And that's what I wanted to experience at that point in my life. I kept my eyes open for an opportunity, and not long after Governor Brown left office, the perfect situation developed—one I could not have foreseen and another example of how fortuitous events have shaped my life.

Years earlier I had made the acquaintance of a serious young man, Nathan Gardels, who had moved to California from the Midwest to become more involved with the anti-Vietnam War movement. But Nathan, the son of a Lutheran minister, was much more of an intellectual than an activist, and as the war wound down, he went back to UCLA and graduated with a degree in Urban Planning. He then parlayed that degree with his political connections and went to work as an advisor for Jerry Brown in Sacramento.

Once Jerry Brown was no longer governor, he seemed ambivalent about what to do with his life. Actually, Jerry Brown has always seemed somewhat ambivalent about what he wants to do, bouncing back and forth between his more spiritual side (he has been both a Jesuit and a Buddhist seminarian) and his political side (three terms as governor, three runs for the presidency, mayor of Oakland, California attorney general). Ultimately, the political side usually wins. Anyway, at that point, Jerry set up a number of nonprofit groups in Los Angeles with various advisors from his administration in order to keep in touch with his important political, business, and intellectual contacts. Nathan Gardels was asked to head Brown's Institute for National Strategy, and it was Gardels' job to nurture Jerry's standing with the "thinking" types.

While Jerry pondered his immediate future, Gardels decided that one of the most effective ways to utilize Jerry Brown's many intellectual/philosophical contacts, both national and international, was to put out a newsletter with articles and interviews with well-known people of influence. He named the newsletter, "New Perspectives." At first, it was a simple, occasional, four-page foldout, printed on rough gray paper, but the content was important and engaging and the newsletter caught on. Gardels saw the potential so he developed the newsletter into a slick, well-designed quarterly journal printed on high-quality paper with fresh and exciting professional graphics. He re-branded the publication as New Perspectives Quarterly (NPQ), and made plans to travel the world interviewing the most influential and respected world leaders, public intellectuals, writers, poets and social theorists he could convince to talk with him. Then, low and behold, Jerry Brown finally decided what he was going to do with his life—he was going to go to Japan and become a Buddhist monk—and Nathan was left holding the bag so to speak because NPQ required, at that point, a considerable subsidy to get off the ground. That's when Nathan showed up at my doorstep.

Well, okay, not literally at my doorstep, and at first, during our discussions, was not clear what he wanted. If I remember correctly, what he actually asked was if we could travel together to Europe because he needed my help in getting an interview with someone I knew. To tell you the truth, I don't really remember exactly how it happened, but I do remember I invited him to our house in Giglio, and we began to talk seriously. He told me about the situation at NPQ, admitted that his trip with me to Italy had used up the last of his funds and asked my advice about how he could raise money for the journal.

"Oh boy," I said. "You certainly hit me at the right time."

"What do you mean?" Nathan asked.

"I've been looking for a project like this. I'd like to get involved."

"Raising money?"

"More than that," I said. "I'd like to help plan where the journal is going, share my contacts for interviews, maybe write a column on the politics of economics…" I was thinking off the cuff, and I could see the wheels churning in Nathan's head.

"Why don't you become the publisher?" he suggested.

"The publisher," I repeated, "uhhh, that has a nice ring to it. I'd like that. I could have my own prestigious journal, a magazine of tremendous influence. I could really make a mark." Nathan looked a little uncomfortable. I realized I sounded like I was taking possession of his baby. "Of course, you would handle the editorial content, Nathan. You will stay the editor, you'd be in control of things. It would be *our* magazine, our journal. *We* can make this happen." He seemed to relax. "So, if I were to be the publisher, what else would that entail?"

"Well," Nathan seemed to hesitate. "There is the issue of money."

"Uhhh, sure, I understand that. No problem. How much do you need?" I was thinking one of the advantages of a quarterly journal was a very small staff, only four issues a year, what could that cost? Couldn't be too much.

"Well, if we give ourselves three years to stabilize, one…maybe one and a half…"

"One hundred fifty thousand, huh?"

"Million, Stanley, one and one half million."

I tried to be nonchalant. "Oh yeah, sure, what was I thinking? I mean we're talking over three years, correct?"

Nathan nodded hopefully.

I was hooked. I wanted to be the publisher of NPQ. "Well, let's do it then." We opened a bottle of excellent chianti and toasted each other as the sun set over the calm Mediterranean Sea below us. But we both must have been very nervous behind our jovial masks. Gardels was out of money, and I was asking myself, where the hell was I going to get that kind of cash for a publishing venture?

When I arrived back in Los Angeles, I had a long talk with Betty. I explained NPQ's situation and told her how much I really believed in the concept. This was my chance to be responsible for one of the premier journals of political and social thought that if Nathan and I were successful, would be read by top academics, opinion makers and policy wonks all over the world. And I would be the publisher. I was very excited.

Betty also loved the idea, but she agreed we didn't have that kind of cash readably available. Just as an aside, Betty and I were, and are, very comfortable, but we don't have the kind of money many folks think we do. Sometimes that's kind of fun, I mean, to be the objects of such wild and inaccurate speculation. However, it wasn't fun when we had something we really wanted to do and didn't have the money to do it. NPQ was something we really wanted to do.

I believe it was Betty who suggested we sell one of our paintings. Betty had always collected art as well as being a working artist, and art was very much a part of the life Betty and I made together. And it was an exciting part of our life. The '50s and early '60s was a time of great transition in art when the center of creativity was passing from Europe, from Paris, London, and Vienna, to New York and Los Angeles. Even before we were married, Betty used to travel to New York, where she would buy paintings from artists she believed in. She had a great eye and great instincts: she purchased a Motherwell, a de Kooning and two or three Pollacks, among others, for a fraction of their eventual value. When we were together, she had a gallery in Santa Barbara that was among the very first in the United States to feature the new artists who were skilled craftspeople working in ceramics, metals, and clay rather than paint. Betty herself worked in metal, and I have wonderful memories of her in her studio wearing her welding mask, blow torch in hand. She looked great. Put the fear of God into me anyway!

So we always had numerous artists hanging around the gallery and our home in Santa Barbara. Then, when we moved to New York, Betty opened a gallery at Madison and 74th which also featured artists from the crafts movement. It was a sensation. When we would have an opening, the gallery had lines that formed all the way around the block waiting to get in. People had never seen this kind of art before and everyone wanted to be associated with this new movement. I loved this part of our lives and at times we both became as wrapped up in the world of art as we were in the world of politics.

As our collection grew we were so proud of each work and so attached to them that we were reluctant to sell anything, but as the years passed, many of those works became more and more valuable and so, from time to time, we would sell a work when we wanted to do something very special.

"What about the de Kooning?" asked Betty. She was referring to *Pink Lady*, one of her most treasured pieces. "That should bring in a substantial amount of cash."

"Oh, uhhh, I don't know, Betty. I…the *Pink Lady*, it's one of your favorites."

"Well, we can put her to work rather than having her sit around the house doing nothing but looking pretty." She smiled at her own joke; deKooning's paintings were seldom if ever described as "pretty." What could I say?

So we put Willem de Kooning's famous *Pink Lady* in auction at Sotheby's, not knowing exactly what she would bring. Boy were we astonished when the top bid reached $3.4 million! That made her my second most favorite famous woman, just below Jean Harlow, but just barely, and my apologies to Barbra Streisand.

So the successful sale of the *Pink Lady* made it possible for me to subsidize the early years of NPQ while Gardels and I set about making the journal a must read for the right people. Nathan was able to use his contacts from the Brown administration and my worldwide network of politicians and intellectuals to develop a series of interviews and articles that truly made an impact and insured NPQ would be demanded in virtually all university libraries, think tanks and upper echelon government offices. We even melded our subscription lists with the remaining supporters of the Center for the Study of Democratic Institutions, and so I was able to give another life to at least the name of the place that had given me so much so many years earlier.

Success built upon success. Gardels argued we should not be bound by our personal politics, and that New Perspectives should uniquely publish the widest range of thought and opinion we could gather together for each issue. In effect, that meant we were always presenting a debate among a number of influential people on a particular topic without regard to their specific positions, or more accurately, because they did have very different positions. Early on, we published articles and/or interviews with, among so many others, President Bill Clinton, King Hussein of Jordan, the influential MIT economist Lester Thurow, Mexican novelist and diplomat Carlos Fuentes, Polish Nobel Prize winning poet Czeslaw Milosz, the futurist Alvin Toffler, Pulitzer Prize winning journalist David Halberstam, novelist and philosopher Umberto Eco, UN peacekeeper Kofi Annan and Secretary of State Henry Kissinger. Before long, our material was being syndicated in major newspapers all over the world through *The Los Angeles Times Global Viewpoint,* and our reputation, as well as a healthy cash flow, was assured. The venture was, and still is, a huge success, and while I am more than willing to give the vast majority of the credit to Nathan

Gardels, my ideas, my behind-the-scenes contacts and financial support, with of course the help of the *Pink Lady*, made *New Perspectives* possible.

Before I move on, there is one story I have to share about Betty's reaction to those early days of NPQ. One of our first major coups was to get an interview with former President Richard Nixon about his opening up diplomatic and trade relations with China. Whatever else one might think about the man, Nixon's China policy has proved an enduring legacy of enormous consequence.

Well, when I showed that issue of New Perspectives to Betty, she hit the roof. "We sold *Pink Lady* to give exposure to that…that crook… that war monger…that…" she sputtered, at a loss for words.

I said, "He's an important man, Betty. We agreed to publish all viewpoints. We've published Kissinger."

"Well," she huffed, "I wasn't very happy about that either. But *Nixon!*"

"The interview was about China. I know you think it's important we've opened up relations with China." Betty and I had, in fact, with our good friend Richard Parker, co-founder of *Mother Jones* magazine and currently a lecturer on Public Policy at Harvard, been part of one of the very first American groups to visit China, and I knew Betty was fascinated with China and Chinese art.

"Yes. I do think Nixon's opening to China was a good thing."

"So, why shouldn't we talk to the man who masterminded that opening?"

Betty still grumbled about the Nixon interview for a long time, but I think it was partially about giving up the *Pink Lady*. Even though she was totally supportive of our investment in NPQ, she really loved deKooning's work.

Eventually Betty and other left-liberal friends came around to accepting that NPQ would often publish individuals and ideas with which we did not agree. But doing so was why we were so much in demand and catalogued by top-ranked universities and institutions. When our success was finally established beyond a doubt, we were bought out by Wiley-Blackwell, the specialty publishers, and as of this writing a subscription to NPQ runs almost $800 per year, $200 per issue. Only Nathan and I ever believed that this was even possible when we had our chat in Giglio.

So, it was around that time, when we were getting NPQ off the ground, that I received the news that Selma, my mother, had died. I did go and see her a few months before she passed away, but things really weren't any better between us. I didn't even go to the funeral. Something was broken inside of me, or her, or perhaps inside of both of us long, long ago and it could not be repaired. Families can be like that.

CHAPTER ELEVEN
Why Don't You Do Right?

You're sittin' there and wonderin' what it's all about. Why don't you do right, like some other men do? "Why Don't You Do Right?," music and lyrics by Kansas Joe McCoy, 1936.

Before I can tell the story of my involvement with the Middle East peace process, I want to explain what being a Jew means to me. I have often said that, although I had my Bar Mitzvah, I was not raised with any real concept of Jewishness as a religious experience. My family, which I gather was pretty typical of many Jewish immigrant families who came to America around the turn of the 20th century, felt a powerful awareness of their cultural and ethnic heritage of being Jewish. This awareness was not, however, really linked to religion or, for that matter, to an identity with the modern state of Israel. In fact, Israel didn't even exist as an independent state in those days, and, unless one's family was in that very, very small minority involved in Zionist politics, and mine definitely was not, Israel was, at best, an historical Biblical land with no meaningful connection to our lives.

Our sense of being Jewish, my sense of being Jewish anyway, came from the Ashkenazi culture, the European Jewish culture, where people spoke Yiddish, not Hebrew, and thought of themselves as Russian or Austrian or Hungarian or German or Polish as much as Jewish, ironic, considering the outcome. This was the culture of the shtetl as celebrated in musicals like *Fiddler on the Roof,* the stories of Isaac Bashevis Singer or the paintings of Chagall. For the most urban and sophisticated, that culture meant the great flowering of Jewish intellectuals, financiers, doctors and scientists in Vienna and Berlin, the

Sigmund Freuds, Albert Einsteins, and Paul Ehrlichs. Well, we all know that great culture perished in the ashes of the Holocaust, but its remnants, so to speak, were re-established in the United States with the European refugees during the '30s and '40s as well as the increasingly educated and sophisticated domestic Jewish population, so that by the time I was rising in power and influence, I must admit that being Jewish in the United States, at least in New York or Los Angeles, was hardly a disadvantage.

Of course there was prejudice. I experienced my fair share directly when I was in Oklahoma and Texas, and we Jews were a distinct minority, wisely on our guard, during the years when I was at Stanford. It would be stupid for me to imply that anti-Semitism has disappeared from the American consciousness, but most of the time, I have not been preoccupied with discrimination. Rather, I have always focused on being extremely proud in all of my political and charitable activities that I'm Jewish because all around me, I have always been involved with so many powerful examples of why I *should* be proud—bright, talented successful Jewish men and women at the highest levels of the arts, business, science, and government. But, to repeat, and frankly, before I became involved in the Middle East peace process, my pride and sense of accomplishment came from my American Jewish culture and its European antecedents, not from any powerful identification with the State of Israel.

One other thing I want to focus on before I tell my stories about Begin and Sharon and Arafat and Rabin and Netanyahu. Sometimes, all of us need to step back and take a moment to look, if only briefly, at a map of the Middle East and nearby environs. Okay, so we see this really, really tiny little country completely, overwhelmingly surrounded by countries hostile to this very small place called Israel. Mostly, we only see the threat, we focus on the threat, and we even see the peace process itself primarily through the lens that it might lessen and someday possibly even eliminate the threat. But let us, for just a moment, think not about threats, but about opportunities, and since I am an economist, economic opportunities. Where does the potential for Israel's future wealth and prosperity reside? In business relationships and trade with the United States? With Europe? No, not really, and less so all the time, as those blocs struggle with their own economic problems. I would argue that Israel's future wealth and prosperity clearly lies in trade and investments in the Middle East, in its own neighborhood, where Israel's advantages and assets can be most effectively leveraged. I firmly believe that eventually Israel will reach an accommodation with its neighbors not for any moral or military reasons, but because it is in its best business interests to do so. It's that simple.

Of course, on the other hand, things are really not that simple; the complexity lies in finding a path to mutual accommodation—a path to peace. And that is how I became involved in the Middle East, by trying to find that first simple trail through the dark forest of war and hatred and treachery toward that larger pathway.

My story actually begins with my friendship with Andreas Papandreou. After we managed to get Papandreou released from detention in a Greek prison in 1968, he was exiled to Sweden. While Papandreou was living in Stockholm, I would visit him, and during these visits, I also met with many of the inner circle of Swedish Social Democrats who were in power at the time including Prime Minister Olof Palme—who would later be assassinated in a murder that remains unsolved to this day—Foreign Minister Sten Andersson, and Secretary General of the Foreign Ministry, Pierre Schori. All of these men, as well as Papandreou himself, were influential members of the Socialist International, an organization with a name that sounds vaguely sinister to American ears, but which is, in fact, merely the worldwide organization of Social Democratic, Socialist and Labor parties. Yasser Arafat, as nominal leader of the Palestinians in exile, was also a member of the Socialist International, and as a result, many of the Social Democratic and Labor politicians in Europe (and elsewhere) had at least a passing relationship with Arafat.

So, in the fall of 1982, when Israeli General Ariel Sharon invaded Beruit, Lebanon, and made his controversial decision to allow right-wing Lebanese militias to enter the Sabra and Shatila Palestinian refugee camps and carry out a massacre against Palestinian fighters, Yasser Arafat was forced to flee from Beirut, and Papandreou, who by then was prime minister of Greece, provide Arafat refuge until another country could be found where Arafat could set up his headquarters. When Arafat disembarked from his plane in Athens, he was greeted with a bear hug by Papandreou and, in a photograph displayed on the front page of The New York Times and other international newspapers, Arafat's pistol is clearly shown protruding from beneath his military-style jacket. This was a public relations disaster for Papandreou who was having serious problems with the US government anyway. The photo only served to convince opponents all over the world that Papandreou was overwhelmingly anti-Israel. I immediately booked a flight from Los Angeles to Athens where I intended to give

Papandreou a piece of my mind for his flagrant disregard for the consequences of his actions.

Eppie On the way to Athens, my flight had to make a connection in New York, so I decided to stay overnight and talk with my friend Arthur Krim about what I was going to say to Papandreou. As it turned out, Krim was already entertaining Ephraim (Eppie) Evron who had been Israel's ambassador to the United States from 1979 to 1982, and before that, a close personal friend of President Lyndon Johnson when Krim was an advisor to Johnson. Anyway, Evron was a very small man with a very big personality, very funny, very out-going, and easy to like. But he totally freaked out when he found out I was going to meet with Papandreou. "How could you, a good Jew, meet with that horrible man?" he asked me.

"Who says I'm a good Jew?" I countered wryly.

Evron didn't miss a beat. "Okay, how come you, a bad Jew, are going to meet with a man who is a sworn enemy of Israel?"

"Papandreou is not an enemy of Israel," I said firmly.

"He's very pro-Arab. Arafat's his good friend!"

"Yes, he is pro-Palestinian. He thinks they got shafted when Israel became a state. He believes Palestinians have been treated very badly by the Israelis. But he's not an anti-Semite."

"Because he's your friend? But you just said you're a bad Jew. Maybe he's only friends with bad Jews?" But he said it with a sparkle in his eyes and a smile forming at the corners of his mouth. I had to laugh.

Eppie and I argued back and forth throughout the evening with Arthur Krim sometimes acting as moderator when things got too heated between us, but as the hours passed I grew to really like Ephraim Evron and I could tell he liked me. Physically, we could not have been more different, I am tall and relaxed, he was short and intense, but by the time the evening ended, we agreed we would keep in touch and share our views about the possibilities for peace in the Middle East. As I became more involved with Palestinians and Israelis over the next fifteen years, Evron's friendship was a great source of comfort for me, particularly when I came under attack. We may have disagreed, but he understood what I was trying to do.

The next day I landed in Athens and had things out with Andreas Papandreou. "What in the hell were you thinking?" I asked him. "That one picture will be used as conclusive proof you are an enemy of Israel."

Papandreou was willing to listen because we had become close friends and because I was instrumental in getting him released from prison, but he was not pleased.

"Oh, come on, Stanley, many, many countries and heads of state asked me to accept Arafat here as a transit point before he goes to Algiers. And he is my friend. He's also the only one who can make peace with Israel."

"But...but," I sputtered, "uh...you didn't have to have your picture taken hugging him with his pistol showing. *Greek Prime Minister Embraces Terrorist!* That's what the headlines said. You could have greeted him in private, Andreas."

"I was not ashamed to greet him, Stanley."

"It's not about shame. You're an extremely intelligent man, Andreas. You know it's about perception. And what about the Americans? You played right into their hands. You know the Americans despise you."

"Hey, you forget I *am* an American citizen, or at least I was until I ran for prime minister of Greece."

"And I think there are many in the US government who hate you even more for having been an American citizen. I think they believe you should be more sympathetic to US requests."

"Stanley, Stanley, you know the US government doesn't request. It demands. I'm tired of it. A lot of us are tired of it. The United States doesn't run the whole world."

"Well," I said, smiling, trying to make a point, "actually, it pretty much does."

We went back and forth like that for awhile, and finally Papandreou more or less agreed that publicly greeting a pistol-packing Arafat might not have been his most astute move. He then asked me, "Since when are you so involved with Israeli issues?"

I told him about my conversation with Ephraim Evron and my recent membership in the ICPME (International Committee for Peace in the Middle East). I expected him to criticize, or at least mildly admonish me. I was actually surprised when he said, "Well, I didn't know you were interested in Israel. And now you know Evron. He's a very important guy in Israel. Nurture that relationship. It might come in handy some day."

The next morning I returned to the United States, and over the next few years I finally began to take more notice of just how serious the problems in the Middle East were. Then Betty and I made a trip to Israel, Jordan, Egypt, and the West Bank sponsored by the World Jewish Congress, which wanted me to become a member. It was just before the first *Intifada*—the Palestinian street revolt against authority —began, and our trip was not exactly the glorious homecoming Betty and I had anticipated. There was tension in the air everywhere, obviously between Arabs and Israelis, but also between the old kibbutzim Israelis and the new urban Jews, between Sabras—those born in Israel—and new immigrants, between the Ashkenazi European Jews and the Sephardic Middle Eastern and North African Jews. I could see that things were going to blow up, and I feared for the future.

Then, not long after Betty and I returned from that trip, I got a phone call from the Swedish diplomat, Pierre Schori whom I'd come to know pretty well after we met again at Papandreou's inauguration. After the usual pleasantries, he told me what he really had in mind: "I was speaking with Andreas about the Palestinian issue, about how we could get peace talks started, or at least how we could get things moving forward because our Foreign Minister Sten Andersson has received signals from Arafat that he, Arafat, might be willing to make certain overtures if the right setting could be found."

I was cautious. "Okay, but how do I fit into this? Shouldn't you be talking to the Israelis."

"There are many reasons, including his own personal safety, why Arafat can't meet with the Israelis, but he might be able to meet with, say, a large delegation of prominent American Jews."

"In order to…?

"Make a statement."

"And that statement would be…?"

"I am not guaranteeing anything, Sheinbaum, but we have been led to believe the statement could be made in public and could include language recognizing the State of Israel's right to exist as well as renouncing terrorism."

"Are you certain?"

"No. With Arafat, nothing is ever certain. We are just feeling our way here. Exploring possibilities, shall we say."

"Uh…well then. I could also explore possibilities. I take it you would like me to form this group of prominent American Jews."

"Would you?"

"It won't be easy, but yes…well, I don't know. I'll make some calls. I'll get back to you."

I was actually very excited by the prospect of putting together a group that could meet with Arafat and witness such an important statement, but the *Intifada* had exploded by that time and feelings against Yasser Arafat, especially within America's Jewish community, were extraordinarily hostile.

Now I had a theory about the *Intifada*, not widely held then but somewhat more acceptable today, which was that the uprising represented the revolt of Palestinian youth against *all* authority, Palestinian as well as Israeli. I felt the young people were also upset with Arafat because twenty years of terrorist warfare had brought them absolutely nothing. Their message was, we need to change tactics, we need to try something different. I also felt that if I was right, or even partially right, the pressure on Arafat to open up some sort of negotiations with the Israelis was percolating toward the boiling point. It was in fact a good time to meet with Arafat and try to push things forward.

But first of all, I had to reduce European expectations that a large group would be desirable. Europeans have a tendency toward large committees where many different viewpoints argue for long periods of time in order to eventually reach a group consensus. My experience was that Americans work better in smaller groups of well-selected people. That sort of group would serve the purpose and be far easier to bring together and keep together through the difficult and sometimes disappointing negotiations. I suggested a group of five members and the Europeans agreed to go along with that number.

So, I started calling around and I did get turned down by a number of people, but eventually I found four distinguished American Jews who agreed to go to Stockholm and meet with Arafat if we were reasonably certain he would actually come to the meeting prepared to accept Israel's right to exist and to renounce terrorism. Our gang of five included: Rita Hauser, a prominent Republican and former United States Ambassador to the United Nations Commission on Human Rights, who, because she was a Republican and a conservative we suggested as our chair; Menachem Z. Rosensaft, a New York attorney and the founding chairman of the International Network of Children of Jewish Survivors, and national president of the Labor Zionist Alliance, a man with impeccable Zionist credentials; Drora Kass a New York psychologist and writer with a long history of interest in Israeli/Palestinian relations; Abraham Udovitch, a prominent Princeton professor of Jewish Civilization in the Near East who had written numerous books about Israel and the Palestinians and who spoke Arabic fluently; and me.

We intended to complete our preliminary discussions through the Swedes in complete secrecy. Because of the highly sensitive nature of what we were proposing to do, we were almost certain that the Israelis and/or the American government would somehow put the kibosh on what amounted to private diplomatic initiatives. At the time I thought we were being incredibly clever and that we succeeded in keeping everything secret. However, from my perspective now, I wonder if the American government and the Israeli government weren't fully aware from the very beginning that we were setting up the meeting with Arafat, and they unofficially wanted to see what would happen. After all, these negotiations were occurring during the later years of the Reagan Administration, and Rita Hauser had important contacts with the upper levels of that administration, especially Secretary of State George Schultz. And I, for my part, had talked about a possible Arafat meeting when I met with my newfound friend Eppie Evron who was part of the Israeli Foreign Service and had links to their intelligence network. He swore he wouldn't reveal the contents of our conversations, but that doesn't seem plausible to me now. So, I'm fairly certain that there must have been some sort of tacit approval from both governments to allow the meeting to go ahead and to see what would come out of it.

For the longest time, there was very real doubt whether any meeting would even take place. Arafat, apparently, truly wanted the meeting to happen, but he had to balance any overtures he might make with the likelihood that since any such statement would shift the official Palestinian policy on Israel and terrorism, he would thus ignite a firestorm in the radical Palestinian community. And after he maneuvered his way through all that, although it had been implied that the Americans would be responsive and would open a dialogue with the Palestinians, it was by no means assured. So Arafat was delaying and changing plans while he tried to build whatever support he needed to be able to make his statement.

Meanwhile, frankly, we were also having trouble on our end. I knew it was terribly important that we have some sort of official-looking paper that said we represented, or were at least known to, American interests. Eventually I dropped any pretense of secrecy, and tried to get a letter from Secretary Schultz that the administration would seriously review the results of or talks with Arafat. Schultz at first seemed willing, then he said no. Firmly. Finally it was Colin Powell, who was Bush Sr.'s National Security Advisor, who provided me with a letter on White House stationary that I intended use to help convince Arafat at our first meeting that our little group was worth talking to.

Just after I solved the credibility problem, a few days before our first meetings in Stockholm's five-star Grand Hotel, Rita Hauser suddenly decided that she wasn't going to be involved because she had become convinced that nothing would come of the process. I was suspicious about her reason. At that point, everyone in the Bush administration must have known the meeting was scheduled, and I was afraid they were trying to stop the meeting by using Rita Hauser. I was also very upset because we had gone through a very specific series of conversations to get Rita committed, and I felt she could not possibly back out when we were getting so close. After much annoying nitpicking back and forth, Rita finally agreed to come to Sweden for the first set of meetings with Arafat and his aides in order to map out the general tone of Arafat's statement.

The negotiations during those first meetings were cordial. Arafat could be, and was, very charming and gracious although he was typically very evasive as to what exactly he was willing to say. He was clearly nervous about taking the risk, and curious about what the benefits would be if he did recognize Israel's right to exist and renounced terrorism. Our group also felt we were each taking personal risks to our reputations simply by meeting with him, and we wanted a clear understanding of how far Arafat was willing to go before we all went public. Finally, we felt we made enough progress in those first meetings that we could adjourn for ten days and then meet again for the final statement and press conference, so we all went home.

Then, just before we were scheduled to fly back to Stockholm, Rita Hauser again called me and said she wasn't going to go to Sweden.

I was furious. I don't usually lose it, but I did lose it with Rita that time. Betty told me she could hear me yelling all the way from the other end of the house. I won't try to reconstruct the conversation because I was so angry that I'm sure I said things and used language that I would prefer not to see written down. But no matter what I said, Rita was adamant. She wasn't going to Sweden to meet with Arafat again. I slammed down the phone and called Ulf Hjertonsson, the Deputy Chief of Mission at the Swedish Embassy in Washington.

"Rita Hauser just told me she won't go back to Stockholm," I told him.

"Are you certain?" said Hjertonsson.

"She seemed pretty certain to me," I said.

"But why?" asked Hjertonsson.

"Her stated reason is that she's convinced nothing will come of these meetings. If there are other reasons, she hasn't mentioned them."

I hesitated, "Look, would you consider going up to New York to talk to her. Tell her Arafat will definitely show up in Stockholm, and he will definitely make the statement we hope he will make."

"Do we really know that for sure?" asked Hjertonsson.

"Of course not. We don't know anything for sure when it comes to Arafat," I said, "but if Rita Hauser backs out, I do know for sure the press conference will never take place and Arafat won't make any statement. Rita Hauser is our nominal chair. She has to be there."

Hjertonsson said, "Okay, I will go up to New York and talk to her."

I guess I'll never know exactly what Hjertonsson told Hauser, but she did agree to go to Sweden. So there we all were, staying in the same luxury Grand Hotel, but when we passed each other in that beautiful plush lobby, we were barely cordial. It was difficult.

And to add to the pressure, we still weren't absolutely certain Arafat would show for the press conference, and if he did, what the exact wording of his statement would be. But the next morning, as I sat nervously in the Swedish Parliament Building waiting for Arafat to appear, suddenly there he was—short, chubby, scraggly beard, black and white Palistinian *keffiyeh* draped over his head, oversized black horn rimmed glasses, olive green military jacket and slacks. The cameras were whirring. There were bright lights everywhere. Arafat was blinking into the cameras and smiling. I knew this was what we had all worked for, and that we would succeed in finally getting talks going between Palestinians and Israelis no matter how long it would take make real progress. I was ecstatic, absolutely overwhelmed. It was a big, big day, although I could not entirely ignore my foreboding that there was trouble ahead.

CHAPTER TWELVE
The Circle Game

We can't return, we can only look behind from where we came and go round and round and round in the circle game. "The Circle Game," music and lyrics by Joni Mitchell, 1970.

I eventually came to like Yasser Arafat. In all my meetings with him, he never failed to listen, to give his own opinions without being strident or aggressive about them, to be polite, charming, even gracious. Yes, he was a tenacious fighter for his people, and yes, he caused a lot of pain to the Jewish people at the very moment when we were suffering from the greatest tragedy in our long history of suffering. I do believe that Arafat also believed the Holocaust was a horrendous event in human history, but I believe that he believed there was no justice in making his people pay the most precious price, their lives and their land, for a tragedy that they did not cause to happen. In our many conversations, Arafat did eventually come to accept that the world demanded the Jewish people be given a refuge, that they have a restored homeland, a haven from the Holocaust and a promise such a horror would never happen again. Lastly, I believe for all that, Arafat could never really accept that a Jewish homeland meant so many Palestinians had to lose theirs.

If Arafat was difficult in any way, it was that in balancing the demands and desires of so many disparate elements in the Palestinian resistance, from the ultra-radical terrorists like George Habash's Popular Front for the Liberation of Palestine which specialized in airline hijackings on one flank, to Palestinians who remained in Israel and sat in the Israeli parliament—the Knesset—on the other, he was often very evasive and unwilling to be tied down to a clear and specific proposal. Our own ethnic prejudices tend to attribute this quality to an Arab personality trait—that Arabs are wily, slippery and untrustworthy. My own experience would attribute this trait more accurately to the inherent personalities of politicians, even some who are my good friends. And Yasser Arafat was, above all else, a politician.

So, in the Parliament building in Stockholm, as Arafat began to speak, to make his statement before the cameras accepting Israel's right to exist and renouncing terrorism, I made it a point to study the reactions of Abraham Udovitch, the one member of our group who understood Arabic fluently. As Arafat launched into the substance of his statement, I could tell Udovitch was not pleased. I whispered in his ear. "Is he saying the wrong things?"

Udovitch whispered back, "No, no, not the wrong things, but he's not exactly saying the right things either."

"What's the problem?"

"Well, he *is* being accommodating, but I do not think the language he is using will be acceptable to the Israelis...or even the Americans. I really do not think so."

Well, I'm not certain that anything Arafat would have said at that press conference in Stockholm would have been acceptable to the Israelis or Americans because to accept Arafat's statement would have meant the respective governments would have had to accept Arafat as a partner in Middle East negotiations and the Israelis and the Americans were not prepared, at that point in time, to do that. I was determined that if Arafat's verbal statements were dismissed as inadequate, we would need to get some sort of commitment in writing that would make things absolutely clear.

However, in the moment, it was excitement and congratulations all around. I remember I stood next to Arafat, towered over him actually, and put my arm around his shoulder, proud that he had shown the courage to make a breakthrough declaration. At that moment, dozens of cameras snapped the photo of me and Arafat, and I remember thinking, oh boy, what will friends back home say when they see this picture?

After the photo session, I was able to speak briefly with Sten Andersson. I immediately questioned him on how he thought Arafat's statement would be perceived.

"It's everything we wanted," he said. He was beaming. "I think now we can arrange to have him appear before the United Nations and make the same declaration."

"But," I said, "Udovitch, who speaks Arabic, says Arafat used deliberately vague language. Won't this be a problem?"

"Perhaps," said Andersson. "Frankly, language can always be seen as a problem. But if Arabic speakers say he was too vague, I promise we will get things in writing before his U.N. appearance. And I will encourage him *strongly*," a wry smile appeared at the corners of Sten's mouth, "to stick to the text in New York."

That was the attitude I liked to hear. That's what the Swedes were all about—*let's get this done*. They wanted to get the peace process moving forward; they weren't going to be deterred by distractions over precise meanings. That was my attitude as well.

But there were many, on all sides of the Israeli/Palestinian debate who were determined to throw up distractions, and so Arafat's statement in Stockholm was dismissed as inadequate by Israel and those supporting Israel, and as a sell-out by radical Palestinian groups and those who supported them. Sometimes being smack-dab in the middle is not the best place to be. Or maybe it was.

The Swedes were successful in urging the United Nations to invite Arafat to speak and repeat his declaration that Palestinians recognize Israel's right to exist and they renounce terrorism as a weapon. However, the Europeans immediately ran into a road block when the United States refused to grant Arafat a visa to come to New York and appear before the United Nations. This was during the waning days of the Reagan Administration, and they were certainly not going to get embroiled in a tug-of-war with Israel at that point. Furthermore, the State Department under George Schultz was particularly pro-Israel, and refusing Arafat a visa appeared to be a relatively easy way to earn Israeli appreciation. Instead, against all expectations, the move backfired.

At the UN, officials decided that if Arafat wasn't going to be allowed to come to speak in New York, then the UN Security Council would pack up and go to meet Arafat in Geneva. I tried to head things off at the pass. I called Rita Hauser and asked her to get in touch with George Schultz. Nothing happened. I tried to reach Schultz myself through congressional contacts, but to no avail. The Administration wouldn't budge. So the UN did have an extraordinary session in Geneva, and Arafat did speak. This was truly an extraordinary move, virtually without precedent, and the UN's willingness to defy the United States and meet with Arafat in Geneva was arguably the single most dramatic public relations coup for the Palestinians in their struggle for recognition.

In his speech on the 13th of December, 1988, Arafat repeated in more precise language the statements he had made in Stockholm, which had been endorsed by the Palestine National Council. He also repeated his demand that there be recognition of a State of Palestine with Jerusalem as its capital and he reaffirmed the right of the refugees to return to their land. Then, the following day, there was a separate statement in which Arafat also expressed a desire for all the states of the region to enjoy peace, security and stability, and he condemned terrorism in any form. In response, and to my surprise, within days, the Reagan Administration, judging I assume that they'd fumbled the ball on this one, agreed to open a substantive dialogue with the PLO. I breathed a huge sigh of relief. Our hard work had paid off big time!

I want to emphasize that although the dividends of the Stockholm and Geneva statements seem somewhat lost and obscure today amidst the ongoing, circular round and round apparently never-ending turmoil in the Midde East, Arafat's statements really were the first tentative steps toward what I still believe will be an eventual peace agreement between Palestinians and Israelis, even if it does not happen in my lifetime.

Furthermore, there were many Israelis who supported my initiatives. Even today, despite the rightward tilt in Israeli public opinion concerning negotiations with the Palestinians, it is still far more acceptable in Israel to hold progressive views on the necessity of negotiations than it is among the vast majority of American Jews. This has always seemed strange to me. I have been over and over that strange dichotomy in my head, late at night, while I'm pondering things. My musings have still reached no conclusion, and I still cannot explain why American Jews take such intransigent positions when it comes to the Palestinians.

Of course, there were also Israelis who vehemently opposed our efforts. And then, there were other Israelis who did not support what I was doing but believed if something good could come out of my efforts, then I should continue my involvement with Arafat. Among those was my friend Eppie Evron. Because he was an influential member of the Israeli government, his support for me personally, if not always of my tactics, was a tremendous source of confidence as I worked to build relationships. On the eve of our press conference in Stockholm, I had checked with Eppie to hear his views on how the Israelis would react. He spoke cautiously: "Publicly? Well, publicly we will condemn his statements as insincere and inadequate. Privately…"

"What? What will the government think privately?"

"I really can't say, Stanley. The Israeli government, even the cabinet, always contains, as you know, a fairly wide range of opinions. Depending on what Arafat is actually prepared to say and on how his own factions react to his statements...then...well...maybe..." Ironic, I thought to myself, and they accuse Arafat of being evasive. Still, it was clear to me that at least some influential Israelis saw the possibility of an opening.

After Geneva, I checked in with Evron again. "Why couldn't Israel give a more positive response, Eppie?

"Be patient, Stanley. You got the Americans to agree to open discussions with the PLO. That's a big step. Let's see where things go with the new president."

Well, the new President was George Herbert Walker Bush so I didn't foresee enormous progress in the works, but one always has to have hope when it comes to peace negotiations.

Meanwhile, things weren't going so well back in Los Angeles. The photo of me with my arm around Arafat's shoulder had appeared on the front page of *The Los Angeles Times* as well as *The New York Times* and there was a huge uproar in the Jewish community. I admit I felt a little more sympathy for what had happened to Papandreou years earlier, except that in my case, I had assumed that helping to bring Arafat into peace negotiations might be welcomed by American Jews concerned about Israel's long-term security. This was definitely not the case, except for a very few exceptions.

The worst agitators to attack me personally were our own little thugs from Rabbi Meir Kahane's notorious Jewish Defense League, ostensibly an organization to actively defend Jewish interests worldwide, but in fact a violent organization with an alleged history of brutal intimidation and political killings in Israel and the United States. Its Los Angeles chapter at that time included a pinhead by the name of Irv Rubin, who was implicated although never charged in the assassination of Alex Odeh, the west coast regional director of the American-Arab Anti-Discrimination Committee. Rubin was also the national director of the Jewish Defense League, and he later committed suicide in jail where he was awaiting trial on charges of conspiracy to bomb private and government property.

In early January of 1989, Rubin and his gangsters delivered a very special New Year's present for Betty and me. When I awoke early on that chilly California winter morning, it was still dark outside. I puttered around in my office, made a few phone calls to Europe and the east coast, and then as the sun rose behind the eucalyptus trees, I looked out the front window and noticed something strange, something unusual on the driveway near the front gate. I couldn't tell what it was so I wrapped my old bathrobe tightly around me and went to investigate. When I got close enough to see what it was, I recoiled in shock. Someone had pitched a skinned pig's head carcass over our gated wall and the bloody mess lay oozing brains and cartilage onto the concrete.

My first reaction was to immediately understand, even though I was not observant, the significance of throwing a pig's head onto a Jew's property. Wow, I thought, what right-wing Nazi freak is pissed at me now. Then I remembered that famous scene in *The Godfather* movie when the mobster finds a severed horse head in his bed and he knows it was placed there by fellow mobsters in order to intimidate him. That's when I understood no Nazi had done this. Only another Jew would think to throw pork on my drive. It had to be Irv Rubin and his boys.

Of course, when I told Betty, we both knew what Rubin was telling us, and it did send shivers down my spine. I asked Betty if she thought we should leave town for a few days.

Betty was defiant. "Hell no," she said, "I'm not going to let those bullies push us around. I'm calling the police."

"That might make things worse," I said. "The newspapers will find out and we'll just give that beast Rubin more attention. That's what he wants."

"Then we'll give him more attention and expose him for the creep he really is."

She did call the cops, and when the local television station KCBS revealed that they had off-camera audio of Rubin saying he would be, "...delivering a huge pig to Stanley Sheinbaum's home," Commander Booth with the LAPD announced that the police, "Based on the tapes that we've seen and the audio we've heard, [would] certainly have to talk to Irv Rubin," and that they were "viewing it as a hatred incident." Of course, nothing was ever proven, but we got Rubin's message, and we knew we were being targeted.

It's a particularly weird feeling to be a Jew terrorized by fellow Jews. There were hostile, malicious phone calls, some in the middle of the night. Invitations to events were cancelled. We would attend charity functions and friends, fair weather friends anyway, would turn the other way, refuse to shake hands. Even close friends were highly critical in private. I remember one long-time, very liberal, very close friend losing his temper and screaming at me that I "was a traitor to my people" in the kitchen of his home while others at a party in the next room listened to his rant.

When we were back home, I spoke to Betty about what was happening. "It's tough," I said, "much tougher than I ever dreamed it would be. Even our friends…"

"We're the tough ones, Stanley, We've been through this before. Remember when you ran for Congress up in Santa Barbara?"

"Yeah, that's true."

"And when the ACLU defended the Nazi marchers in Skokie?"

"Right. Yeah. I remember."

"And when you organized Ellsberg's defense."

"Okay, okay, Betty. I get it."

"It's the pattern of our lives, Stanley. We do not choose the easy path. You have become a well-known public figure despite your efforts to operate behind the scenes. You bring people together. Sometimes they don't want to be brought together. Sometimes they're going to get angry."

"I know. But I just get so tired of all the anger and bitterness when I'm only trying to promote some sort of dialogue. I'm exhausted. I wish we could spend more time at our house in Italy, on Giglio. I wish…"

Betty ignored me. "You know, Stanley, you've received a number of requests to appear at various synagogues to talk about your relationship with Arafat. Maybe we should accept some of these invitations and you can explain what you are trying to accomplish by being involved in the peace process."

We did. The first engagement was with a congregation at a synagogue in the San Fernando Valley. Frankly, I don't remember which one, and I suppose I don't really want to remember. It was a horrible experience. The Rabbi had no sooner introduced me and I had begun my talk when the yelling, the invective, the fists raised in anger, the name-calling started. I tried to move on, but I could not speak over the raised voices so I nodded to Betty and we left.

In the car, I looked at Betty. "Well, that was a huge success," I said.

She noted my sarcasm. "I don't think they liked you very much, Stanley."

"No, they didn't. Why are we doing this?"

She ignored me. "There's a synagogue in Beverly Hills, on Burton Way, Temple Emanuel. They might be more receptive. At least I think they will listen."

A few weeks later, we arrived at the front door of Temple Emanuel. There was a considerable crowd gathered outside the temple, and there was some pushing and shoving going on. Honestly, I was more than a little apprehensive. When Betty and I moved toward the front door and people stepped back to make way for us, I glanced over my shoulder and saw a half dozen unpleasant looking men in some sort of uniform lining up behind us. As we moved forward through the doors into the temple, they marched in a column behind us. Suddenly it dawned on me, these were the notorious JDL storm troopers, and I use that description deliberately, because that's what they were. They followed us all the way down the aisle to the front row where they sat, grimly, sullenly, as the Rabbi made his introduction and asked for the traditional Jewish attitude of tolerance while I made my presentation.

When I began to speak, I looked down at those pretentious gangsters in the first row and made eye contact with each of them. I let my contempt show through. Suddenly, I was not afraid anymore.

I expected another tumultuous meeting, but actually things went rather well. Sure there were some in the crowd who asked questions belligerently, but most of the questions were thoughtful, curious, and in all cases people let me explain my position. There was no name calling, no shouting. Even though our pathetic storm troopers frowned and grimaced there in the first row, they kept their mouths shut.

After I was finished speaking, members of the congregation brought Betty up next to me, and there was, not enthusiastic, but still polite applause. Then the rabbi whispered, "follow" and he led Betty and me through the back of the sanctuary to a rear door. He shook my hand as we left and said to me, "Thanks for coming, Stanley. I do not agree with what you are doing, but I do admire your courage." He turned toward Betty. "And you as well, Betty. Shalom."

That experience and others gave me some hope that the reaction to my meeting with Arafat would eventually calm down, but I was to find that, to the contrary, animosity for what I had done continues to this day, and I've come to the conclusion that I will face hostility from many in my own community until I'm finally gone for good.

CHAPTER THIRTEEN
I Didn't Know What Time It Was

Didn't know what year it was, life was no prize....I'm wise, and I know what time it is now. "I Didn't know What Time It Was," lyrics by Lorenz Hart, music by Richard Rogers, 1939.

After the Stockholm and Geneva declarations, the peace process did move forward in fits and starts, three steps forward, two steps back, that sort of thing. My greatest positive feelings about the declarations came from the fact that American policy appeared to move significantly in favor of talks with Arafat and the PLO. My greatest disappointment came when the American Jewish Congress published an analysis of the Stockholm and Geneva declarations and concluded that there was nothing new in what Arafat said. I was furious because their analysis was such a ridiculous propaganda effort to stall negotiations. Again, mainstream American Jews were muddying the waters to what purpose? Arafat was clearly willing to make concessions. Even the Americans were willing to talk to Arafat. I felt it was time for American Jews to move beyond their intransigence and be open to positive signs that something could be accomplished if we would all try harder and be open to change.

The Bush Administration, the George Herbert Walker Bush Administration with James Baker as Secretary of State, turned out to be more willing to work for peace than I had initially assumed. In 1989, Baker spoke before a meeting of AIPAC (the American Israel Public Affairs Committee, a very pro-Israel lobbying group) during which he signaled that the American government was shifting from the policies of the Reagan Administration, which had been unusually pro-Israel, to a more balanced position. What happened, basically, was that Bush Sr.'s quick victory in the First Gulf War was seen as an opportunity to establish a new order in the Middle East. However, the first Bush Administration also realized that a key element in establishing this new order dominated by American power remained a peace treaty between Israel and the Arab states. That could only be established in conjunction with successful negotiations between Israel and the Palestinians.

By the fall of 1991, the United States had moved to the point where it co-sponsored, with the USSR, a conference in Madrid hosted by the Spanish government that brought together the Israelis and various front line Arab states including Syria, Jordan and Lebanon to create a framework for more detailed negotiations between Israelis and Palestinians. Theoretically and for public consumption, the Palestinians were not directly involved in these negotiations, but in reality, representatives of the Palestinians were present and consulted. As a side point, I've always found it interesting to note that this was the last major conference sponsored by the Soviet Union, which fell apart at almost the same time as the conference was taking place. Russia, however, also continued to be involved in seeking a peace agreement.

Progress in Madrid led to the Oslo Accords, the supposedly "secret" agreements worked out in the summer of 1993, which were the first acknowledged face-to-face discussions between Israelis and Palestinians. The accords were meant to establish a framework of principles for all future negotiations. At the time, it appeared that they would. Everyone was very upbeat. Betty and I were invited to attend the official signing ceremony at the White House hosted by President Bill Clinton on September 13, 1993.

Just before the ceremony itself, Betty and I were mingling among various invitees, including a number of American Jews from Los Angeles who were hostile as hell toward me for my meetings with Arafat. I was feeling a little apprehensive, a little downbeat even though I was excited about the event itself. I remember I turned to Betty and remarked, "I don't get the feeling we're too popular with this crowd."

"Ignore them, Stanley."

"They used to be friends. They've been to dinner at our house."

"Forget about it, dear. This is a big day. Let's enjoy it." She squeezed my arm. "Look there's Colin," she added.

Colin Powell was, at that time, still the chairman of the Joint Chiefs of Staff under President Clinton. Seeing him cheered me up a bit. After all, it was Colin Powell who provided me with that letter on

White House stationary that I used to help convince Arafat at our first meeting back in Stockholm that our little group was worth talking to. I hadn't spoken to General Powell since then, and I looked forward to seeing him.

Well, just as the ceremony was beginning, Powell joined with the other dignitaries around the dais, and as he moved forward, he catches my eye, smiles, points at me and yells out, "Hey, you started all this!" You could almost hear jaws drop in the we-hate-Sheinbaum section of the crowd, but I have to admit I was so pleased to be recognized for my contribution on this historic occasion. Suddenly, I felt great, and decided Betty was right—to hell with all those who were bent on running me down. Betty whispered in my ear, "See, Stanley, there are some pretty important people who understand and appreciate all you have done."

Then, after various speeches, the famous picture was taken where Yitzhak Rabin and Yasser Arafat reached across to each other and shook hands while President Clinton stood behind them, arms outstretched, to join the three of them together in a mutual gesture of peace making. I tell you, it brought tears to this old Jew's eyes. I was often so pessimistic that I would ever see that day.

And then, just as those feelings of hope and opportunity filled the diplomatic air, they were all blown away by the senseless act of that little right-wing madman, not an Arab, not a German, not an Iranian, but a fellow Jew—Yigal Amir. I will never, never understand how Rabin could have been assassinated in public by an Israeli in Israel. Never. But I have to admit, in a very perverted sense, the assassination accomplished its purpose because after Rabin's death, Israeli politicians understandably assumed that the risks of compromise with Palestinians might involve threats to their own lives. And in general, in Israel, with the continuing *Intifada* and the Rabin assassination, opinion drifted further and further right against any significant concessions to the Palestinians.

During this time, I made what efforts I could to try and keep peace negotiations on track, but, of course, I couldn't accomplish much in that poisoned environment. Furthermore, back here in the United States, Clinton was preoccupied with his political troubles after the Monica Lewinsky affair. However, when we spoke, President Clinton still expressed great interest in pursuing peace negotiations, so I continued to do what I could. I made a trip to Damascus and was warmly received by Hafez al-Assad. We talked about the possibilities for a peace agreement with Israel, but discussions always circled back around to the Palestinians. Could Israel make an agreement with the Palestinians? Would the United States be willing to pressure Israel? I said, truthfully, that I didn't know the answers to those questions, although I tried to remain optimistic.

I also made a number of trips to Jordan and got to know King Hussein and Queen Noor. There I was, Stanley K. Sheinbaum meeting with an Arab king and his beautiful American-born queen. Boy, if my mother could have only seen me then. Well, maybe it wouldn't have mattered. Maybe she would have just said, "Stanley, why are you wasting your time with those people?" Anyway, the King and Queen were a delightful couple, and they were truly committed to peace with Israel. King Hussein was, after all, the second Arab head of state to formally recognize Israel, but he too could only move so far. We often forget roughly half the population of Jordan is of Palestinian origin, and there has been more than one bloody Palestinian uprising against the monarchy.

Since Queen Noor was American-born and a recognized world leader in humanitarian causes, I found it easy to talk to her. I thought I might be able to persuade her to convince her husband to get more involved in the peace process. She was sympathetic. She indicated she also wanted him more involved.

"Then what can I do to help?" I asked her.

"You have access to Bill Clinton. Can't he get the Israelis to make significant concessions? I swear to you, Stanley, if the Israelis would only bend a little more, they would get a positive response." She was probably right, but the weakened Clinton presidency made really bold moves virtually impossible. It seemed that all the major players truly wanted peace, but for various reasons they were locked in place unable to make the moves each knew were necessary to get the process moving again.

I also met with Arafat at his compound in Ramallah once he had been allowed to return from exile in Algiers to the West Bank. On one occasion, Betty traveled with me. We landed at Ben Gurion International Airport near Tel Aviv and immediately transferred to a car for the drive southeast into the desert which Israelis refer to as Judea and Samaria and the Palestinians as the occupied territories. As we approached the border the land grew hotter, dustier and less developed, the roadway rougher, bumpier. We then had to wait at one of the infamous checkpoints before we could enter the West Bank.

The checkpoints were truly chaotic. There were hundreds, perhaps thousands, of Palestinians attempting to either travel into Israel or back into the Palestinian territories. Old and young, mothers with crying babies, mothers with patient babies, old men bent and gaunt, young men going to or coming back from work. The line didn't seem to move at all. As we entered the checkpoint, I was focused on one young woman carrying a very small infant as the soldiers went through her belongings. She didn't appear angry or upset, instead there was a look of resignation as she pressed her child against her chest.

We were fortunate that we could enter the line for foreign visitors, especially fortunate when we produced US passports, most fortunate that we were met by one of the chief Palestinian negotiators, a major figure in the Palestinian Authority, Nabeel Shaath. Shaath smoothed everything out with the Israeli soldiers manning the checkpoint, although we could see the young soldiers shaking their heads while they looked at our car as if to say, what are you fools doing?

As our convoy moved forward, one of the soldiers looked inside an open window and stopped our progress. I leaned forward toward him. My movements seemed to spook him a bit. His grip tightened on his gun. "It's all right," I said, trying to be helpful, "we have an appointment to meet with Yasser Arafat."

Now the soldier was really spooked. "You're Americans? Why would you want to meet with Arafat?"

Shaath leapt out of his car and hurried back toward us. He handed the soldier official papers which seemed to clear up the delay. After awhile, we were moving forward again.

As we sped off toward Ramallah, I happened to again see the young mother with her baby, still being questioned at the checkpoint, still holding her child tightly against her chest.

The roads on the Palestinian side were in even worse shape as we drove toward Ramallah. Unpaved, potholed gravel highways, the dust rose and swirled in our wake as we passed goat herds, olive trees, rock strewn hillsides. As we rounded a bend in the road, we were able to see what looked like a makeshift village built from all sorts of discarded cinderblocks, tin roofs, plastic tarps, sprawling up a hillside, mules and carts in the streets jockeying for position with motorbikes spewing blue acrid smoke. Children played along the side of the road. "What is this place?" asked Betty. I shrugged; I didn't know.

"One of the refugee camps," our driver said over his shoulder as he kept his eye on the road and his hands firmly on the steering wheel while we bounced across yet another series of potholes.

"My God," mumbled Betty, "oh my God," she said over and over again. She didn't need to explain her reaction. I understood the sadness and disillusionment she was feeling. The camps, originally meant as temporary housing for Palestinians displaced by Israeli troops in the wars for Israeli independence fifty years earlier, were very depressing. They had become semi-permanent wretched hovels filled with people who, by international law, couldn't settle outside their camps and couldn't return to their homes in what had become Israel. Theirs was a limbo with little hope for eventual salvation.

Ramallah itself was fairly good sized, the de facto capital of the Palestinian Authority. It would have been considered a poor, rundown unattractive town if it had been located within Israel itself, but it was fairly well off by Palestinian standards. There were a number of five or six story cinder block apartment buildings with satellite antennas and solar panels on their roofs. In the center of town there were markets bustling with activity and displaying a fairly wide selection of produce, olives, lemons, oranges, tomatoes, and consumer goods—I saw refrigerators, radios, televisions, car parts. The atmosphere was friendly, definitely unthreatening to the point that people were uninterested in who we were or what we were doing.

Arafat's compound the *Muqataa* where he lived and had his headquarters was an exceedingly modest collection of concrete buildings surrounded by ten to fifteen foot walls. I have since read that the Israelis contend that Arafat was in fact a very, very rich man while the Palestinians contend that the funds in banks around Europe and the Middle East, while in Arafat's name, were used for various projects on behalf of the Palestinian people. I really don't know where the truth lies, but I can tell you that Arafat's compound, while reasonably comfortable, was definitely not luxurious by any stretch of the imagination.

When Betty and I met with Arafat, he was gracious and upbeat, presenting us with gifts including a beautiful white mother of pearl box intricately carved and set with different colored sea shells. He wore his signature kefiyyeh—his black and white checkered scarf, but unless I gave him something to read, he did not wear his oversized glasses. He also wore his olive green uniform and his beard was the same scraggly beard he'd worn in every picture I'd ever seen of him, all the way back to when he was a young man.

His health seemed good although his lower jaw quivered a bit when he spoke. He was energetic, but underneath it all I sensed he was nervous, worried, somewhat distracted. Understandable, because negotiations around bringing peace between Israelis and Palestinians were not going well, and he was beginning to lose control of the

Palestinian street while simultaneously being blamed for inspiring the ongoing *intifada*. It was an impossible, no-win situation for him.

We actually spent most of our time reminiscing about when we first met in the snows and cold of Stockholm, Sweden, where we hammered out his positions on recognizing Israel and renouncing terrorism. For some reason I remember I asked him if he liked me then, if he trusted me from the beginning.

"You were very friendly, very warm," he said.

"Well, I was comfortable with you too," I said. "I knew we could get some good work done."

Arafat appeared almost wistful. "We did do some good work. I thought then that by now we could have moved things further along."

"There's still hope, I said.

He wet his lips and looked off into the middle distance, thinking thoughts I'm glad I couldn't know. I repeated myself, "There's still a chance for peace."

Again, he didn't answer me. He turned to Betty. "Your husband is a brave man. He doesn't let anything stop him. I wish there could be more like him."

Betty nodded. "You know," she said to Arafat, "Stanley really does believe peace is possible. He really does."

For the third time, Arafat didn't actually respond, but a sorrowful smile passed across his tired face.

Well, in the years that followed, things got worse for Arafat. He became increasingly isolated. The *Intifada* continued; the violence spiraled. Fences were erected. Jewish settlements spread further and further into the West Bank. Finally, near the end of Clinton's presidency, he brought Arafat and Israeli Prime Minister Ehud Barak together at Camp David to make one last attempt to reach a final status settlement.

According to the historical record provided by Americans and Israelis, Barak offered Arafat the best deal the Palestinians could ever get and Arafat turned it down. The Palestinians, on the other hand, insist to this day that there was no negotiating at all, that Barak and Clinton presented Arafat with a take it or leave it agreement which contained certain provisions that would have been impossible for Arafat to accept. I don't know. I wasn't there. And even though I had contact with both Clinton and Arafat, I have never been sure about what really occurred at Camp David. I can share the fact that Shaath, who was on the Palestinian negotiating team called me one evening in despair.

"They're not really talking to us, Stanley. They're just pushing us around and saying do this, sign that…" his voice wavered somewhere between anger and frustration. I could tell he was almost in tears. He understood what was at stake.

"Nabeel," I said, "I don't know what your bottom line is, but I can tell you, Clinton can't push Barak any further than he has. Remember what happened to Rabin."

"But Stanley, the Israelis aren't offering anything new. Their proposals contain the same things they have always contained. Holbrooke has just repackaged the proposals in new gift paper and he now says we have to accept them. No changes. None."

I knew he was referring to Richard Holbrooke, the US diplomat who had a long history of negotiating Middle Eastern affairs. While Holbrooke was a brilliant, highly respected negotiator, admired by many in the United States, I found him stubborn, arrogant and overly sympathetic with Israeli positions. I feared that if he was the one pushing Arafat around, things would end badly. He was, and they did.

After the collapse of the Camp David talks, the situation in the Middle East went from bad to worse. Clinton left office. George Bush became president. The Iraqis invaded Kuwait; the United States invaded Iraq. King Hussein and Arafat backed the Iraqis. Al-Qaeda struck the World Trade Center and the Pentagon. So much was happening. It seemed that each day brought another source of conflict and increased tension. Eventually, the Israeli army laid siege to Arafat's compound. The walls were breached, most of the buildings were destroyed and although the army knew that international opinion would not allow them to enter the building where Arafat was living under deplorable conditions, they made life hell for Arafat and the few advisors who remained inside with him.

In 2003, Nabeel Shaath was able to come to the US for a visit. He arrived in Los Angeles at the same time Betty had an opening at The Artists Gallery where she was exhibiting her latest paintings. Shaath was gregarious and upbeat when he arrived at our home, but his mood turned despondent once we were alone and able to talk.

"The situation is very, very bad, Stanley. Very bad. Arafat is not well. We don't know what's really wrong with him, but he can't get good medical attention there in what's left of the *Muqataa*. Meanwhile Hamas grows stronger every day. I'm afraid the prospects for peace are really gone. I'm sorry, Stanley. You worked so hard."

Obviously, I did not particularly want to hear that news. I tried to stay upbeat so I suggested we attend Betty's opening since it would be a cheerful event. I rented a big black SUV with darkened windows and managed to use my contacts from when I was a police commissioner to get us a full police escort for our drive to the gallery. We were rumbling through the streets of West LA, sirens blaring, motorcycles in front and back. It was kind of silly in some ways but it made Shaath feel good for awhile.

When we arrived at the opening, the party was in full swing and the gallery was packed. Heads turned to see who was arriving in the big black SUV with a police escort, and I'm sure many people were straining to catch a glimpse of some celebrity they could brag over their evening meals that they had seen at the party. As word slowly spread that the "celebrity" was actually a top official in the Palestinian Authority, the crowd thinned out fairly quickly. I was shocked.

An elegantly dressed, silver-haired woman approached Betty, and confronted her fairly aggressively. "How could you bring a man like that to this opening!"

"Mr. Shaath is a very nice man, a gentleman, he's not causing any trouble." She pointed to the corner where Nabeel was quietly studying one of Betty's beach paintings.

"He's Palestinian, isn't he? A terrorist. I didn't come here to be exposed to this sort of person. You should be ashamed." And with that, she stormed out of the gallery's doors. Fortunately, Nabeel didn't hear her. He seemed unaware that his presence could cause any controversy, and Betty and I didn't say anything to him about what had happened. He had enough on his mind.

Near the end of October, 2004, news came that Arafat had become ill during a meeting and he had vomited profusely. He then agreed to leave the *Muqataa* and go to Paris for emergency medical attention. We knew the situation was dire because Arafat swore he would never leave for fear he would not be allowed back. He was flown on a French government jet to Paris and entered the hospital immediately. His condition worsened, and on November 11, 2004, he died in Paris. His body was returned to Ramallah, and although he had requested, and his family again requested, that he be buried in East Jerusalem, the Israeli government absolutely refused to even consider allowing him to be buried there. And so, Arafat's funeral and burial took place in Ramallah where his tomb is considered a "temporary" resting place until he can be buried in East Jerusalem, as the capital of an independent Palestinian state. The Israelis swear this will never, ever happen.

I was almost broken by Arafat's death. I truly believe, although others disagree, that if he had lived, there was still a path to peace.

That's a big *if* I know. If Rabin hadn't been assassinated. If Arafat had lived. We can change the present, but we can't change history.

After Arafat died, the situation in the Middle East only became more chaotic, the positions of the various parties more extreme. A peace agreement has been my most fervent dream and I have devoted so much of my life to achieving one. My failure is the greatest disappointment I have ever experienced, and I can only take solace from the knowledge that I really, really tried. I really did.

(left) Stanley does his best to make a point with a skeptical Israeli Prime Minister Ehud Barak

(right) Palestinian President Yasser Arafat greets Stanley during negotiations in Ramallah.

(left) Stanley tries to salvage some remaining momentum toward peace with a thoughtful Shimon Peres, ex-Labor Party leader and president of Israel.
(photo: Peter Halmagyi)

(left) Stanley with Leah Rabin, wife of the assassinated Israeli Prime Minister, Yitzhak Rabin.

(left) Stanley with longtime Palestinian negotiator Hanan Ashrawi. Ashrawi is a representative from the once thriving but now dwindling Palestinian Christian community.

(right) Stanley welcomes King Hussein of Jordan to a star-studded event in Sheinbaum's Brentwood home. (photo: Barry Levine)

(left) Stanley with King Abdullah. Upon King Hussein's death, his son, Abdullah, became Jordan's leader.

(right) Stanley with King Hussein of Jordan's American-born wife, Queen Noor.

Stanley meets with another peacemaker, the Dali Lama, to help promote prospects for reconciliation among all the world's peoples.

151

Although Stanley is not particularly known for his efforts to improve US relations with Latin America, he has met with a number of dignitaries to discuss possibilities for greater understanding. (left) Stanley with Nicaraguan President Daniel Ortega for an NPQ interview during Ortega's first term as president. (middle) Stanley meets with President Fidel Castro during a visit to Cuba. (bottom) Stanley in vigorous discussion with the Argentine publisher, journalist, and author Jacobo Timerman (photo:Barry Levine) who was first persecuted and then honored for confronting the atrocities of the Argentine military regime's Dirty War.

152

(left)The Rev Jesse Jackson introduces Stanley at a benefit honoring Stanley's many contributions to promoting civil liberties.

(right) Norman Lear plants a kiss on the cheek of his good friend Stanley as Stanley is honored by the ACLU. (photo: Walter Rayher

(left) Stanley with Police Foundation President Hubert Williams. The foundation's report supported the allegations that there were numerous problems with the administration of LA Police Chief Daryl Gates.

Stanley with celebrities sympathetic to progressive causes: (left) actor Martin Sheen, (photo: Barry Levine) (center) William Morris venerable founder of the legendary William Morris Agency and Mrs. Morris, (photo: Marc Korody) (bottom) international film star Julie Andrews. (photo: Stephanie J. Harker)

(left) Julie Belafonte adjusts Stanley's trademark bow tie as Harry Belafonte approves.

(right) Stanley gets a chance to spend time with controversial filmmaker, the irascible Michael Moore.

(left) Stanley and Betty flank one of their favorite politicians, Vermont Senator Bernie Sanders.
(photo: Stephanie J. Harker)

(left) Gil Sheinbaum (left) with Stanley. The two brothers have become close over the years and enjoy their time together.

(right) Stanley seated with his longtime friends, the Tuesday Knights who have gathered around Stanley's round dining table monthly for more than 25 years: Mike Farrell, Paul Schrade, Fred Nicholas, George Regas, Leonard Beerman, and Dick Gunther.

(left) Betty and Stanley are regarded with obvious admiration and affection by Hollywood superstars and liberal activists Warren Beatty and Annette Bening. (photo: Cathy Blaivas)

CHAPTER FOURTEEN
I'll Be Seeing You

I'll be seeing you in all the old familiar places that this heart of mine embraces.
I'll Be Seeing You" lyrics by Irving Kahal and music by Sammy Fain,
1938.

During all those years when I was involved in searching for peace in
the Middle East, during the years when I served on the California
Board of Regents, even when I was president of the Los Angeles
Police Commission, I was still involved in presidential electoral politics,
usually on behalf of the Democratic Party. I wanted to believe the
Democrats remained the party of Roosevelt, committed to relative
economic parity and security for the least advantaged in our society.
That was the national political issue I cherished most, and as an
economist, the one issue about which I was most knowledgeable.

Economics are at the heart of the American experience. Whatever
else this country has stood for, it has always marketed the belief,
illusory or not, that an American is free. And the reward an American
gets from entering into competition, hard work, and persistence is the
possibility that a person can become fabulously rich. The implied
downside of that freedom is that American success is a fierce
competition, and if the free American fails, for whatever reason, well,
hey, that's the breaks. If you don't like it, you can always go suffer
under the Communists or live with the losers in socialist Europe.

Interestingly enough, almost all Americans, rich and poor and in-
between, believe in that economic model—perhaps the poor and the
in-betweeners most of all. That's why Americans have never really had
political parties based on alternative economic models. Republicans

were obviously believers, but Democrats were believers, too. No Socialists. No Communists. Those ideas were un-American.

The Great Depression shook the foundations of that belief in *laissez-faire* capitalism, and the Democrats, by accepting Keynesian economic theories, became the party that promoted a modified, adulterated version of capitalism to provide relief for all those ruined lives. But I stress adulterated. Despite what Republicans say, Keynes was no socialist.

I was a Keynesian Democrat and more or less comfortable in the Democratic Party as it stood from Roosevelt's New Deal through Lyndon Johnson's Great Society. During my time as a fellow at the Center for the Study of Democratic Institutions, Ping Ferry would sometimes argue a more socialist perspective. He would suggest, for example, that we study a national health care system, and Robert Hutchins would sit, cradling his pipe in his hand, looking deeply thoughtful and ask, "Why would we want to study national health care? We will never have such a system in the United States."

Ping would become impatient. "Well, that's the point! Maybe we should."

"But a national health system would be undemocratic." replied Hutchins, calm as ever. "We study *democratic* institutions, Ping."

I would waiver back and forth during these discussions, sometimes supporting Ping and sometimes Robert Hutchins. It eventually occurred to me that the argument was as much about the meaning of the word "democratic" as it was about health care or regulation of markets.

When Al Rubin and I met periodically, he would eloquently defend the socialist position and explain what democracy meant to him. "It's not about freedom or government control, said Al. "Democracy means that citizens participate. Ideally, it means that the citizens actually determine the people and policies that govern them. But if large segments of a population are so disadvantaged that they cannot have meaningful participation, then two things happen: those with the advantages, those with the most money become disproportionately powerful, and everyone else becomes disinterested. They just don't care."

I realized the truth of Al's argument, but there was nowhere to take that argument in mainstream American politics, and I wanted to be involved in mainstream politics even if it was from the liberal-left side of the mainstream.

I started my involvement during the presidential election of 1972. It was easy for me to be very active raising money for a presidential candidate like George McGovern. His courage and his basic intelligence, his lonely, somewhat Quixotic anti-Vietnam War campaign against Richard Nixon, his calm and reasonable demeanor made it easy for me to spend time with him. After the campaign was over, we remained friends and travelled to Africa where we met various heads of state including, most memorably, Julius Nyerere of Tanzania, a passionate advocate of African socialism. He was also one of the rare post-colonial African leaders to voluntarily leave office when voted out.

After McGovern's overwhelming defeat, Democrats turned to an apparent outsider, the governor of Georgia, Jimmy Carter. Betty and I and a small number of our friends met with Carter very early on when no one outside of Georgia knew much about him. Frankly, we were not too impressed. He was very likable, even charming, but he didn't seem to know a great deal about foreign affairs and he appeared somewhat naive about domestic economic issues. However, in the wake of the Watergate scandal, fortune smiled on Mr. Carter. We did eventually support him, and he turned out to be the right man at the right time. Then the gods of politics turned against him with the energy crisis and the Iran hostage situation. By 1980, his presidency seemed ineffective.

Meanwhile the Democratic Party was breaking apart over cultural issues including feminism, abortion, gay rights, race discrimination, environmental concerns, and definitions of patriotism. These issues are important; they're very important. They cannot be compromised. However, these cultural issues divorced from questions of economic inequality, corporate power, and growing income disparity pulled the Democratic Party toward becoming a party of cultural liberalism which provided little or no commensurate economic hope for the working class and middle-class voters who had previously been the Democrats' core constituency.

I actually supported the Rev. Jesse Jackson in the Democratic primary. But when he was defeated by President Jimmy Carter, a number of us from our group nicknamed the Malibu Mafia, supported John B. Anderson, the Republican running as an independent, for president. I felt badly about abandoning Carter, but I was drawn to Anderson when I watched the Republican primary debate in Iowa, and I loved it when Anderson flatly declared that the concept that we could lower taxes, increase defense spending, and balance the budget was simply impossible. No other candidate in that election, nor do I think any candidate since, has had the courage to state that simple fact. To the contrary, both parties, besotted with the nonsense of Reaganomics have declared we can lower taxes, increase defense spending, and balance the budget because lower taxes will lead to greater growth. It's nonsense, but until the Great Recession of 2008, most everyone in politics simply repeated that line as gospel. Anyway, I backed Anderson, although his campaign went nowhere, and Ronald Reagan won.

By 1984, the Democratic Party was clearly chasing the same money sources the Republicans were chasing. I could see the writing on the wall, but my friend George McGovern decided to run one more time so I backed him out of affection and loyalty. By the time it was clear that George's campaign wasn't going to catch on, he'd run up considerable expenses, so he called me to ask for my help.

"I'm getting out, Stanley," he said, "but I've already accumulated over one hundred thousand in debt."

"I can't cover that by myself," I told him, "but I'll throw a large fundraiser at the house and invite Mondale and Hart to speak. We should be able to raise enough money to help pay off some of your loans."

I called Hugh Hefner who not only agreed to come, he also invited his list. Soon the names of those wanting to attend mushroomed beyond the capacity our yard could handle, but we held the event anyway and ended up hosting one of the biggest political fundraisers of that season. Lots of A-listers. So, George received enough money to retire almost all of his campaign debts, and we got a chance to look at Senator Gary Hart and Vice President Walter Mondale up close and personal as they say. I wasn't overly impressed.

Walter Mondale was a good, decent man, heir to the Hubert Humphrey brand of Minnesota liberalism which meant he had some sympathy for, and loyalty to, the unions and working people. But he had no spark, no charisma, and I'm not sure his gut feelings were ever really in the race. Gary Hart was an interesting fellow, bright, articulate, aggressive, but he was flirting with the "new politics" that would eventually become the Democratic Leadership Council, a group that firmly committed the Democratic Party to chasing the same money and supporters the Republicans chased. As a result, I didn't altogether trust him.

Mondale and Hart ran neck and neck in a real horse race which went right up to the convention, at which point Walter Mondale pulled ahead for the right to get stomped by Reagan. In the end, I did support

Mondale, who was probably the last of the old-fashioned liberals, but I was not very enthusiastic.

The problem with those old-fashioned liberals is that they courted labor because they needed the money and the votes labor could bring, but they weren't really interested in arguing against the economic changes that were sweeping the country, nor were they proposing policies that could help working and middle class people. They certainly weren't going to stop the tide of Reaganomics being foisted upon the electorate. They weren't prepared to ask if giving up pensions for the risks of 401ks made sense in the long run. They weren't prepared to argue whether corporate salaries were getting out of line. They weren't prepared to argue the consequences of growing economic disparity. Those were the years when all of this voodoo economics started to take hold, and the Democrats weren't fighting it. They were fighting with each other over cultural politics.

Then, in the 1988 primary, Hart imploded over that idiotic sex scandal with Donna Rice and a luxury yacht...*Monkey Business*, I think. A yacht named *Monkey Business*? What was Hart thinking? So that left the field to Michael Dukakis. He seemed a nice enough guy, but I don't think I ever met him. I didn't raise money for him. I'm sure I voted for him, but by then I was losing interest in presidential politics. I suppose you could accuse me of being the kid on the playground who couldn't get his way, so he took his ball and bat and went home. If the Democrats weren't going to fight against Reaganomics, I didn't want to play with them.

And this was also the time when our group, the so-called Malibu Mafia, began to split apart as we each followed our own interests. Norman Lear, and I honestly mean my dear friend Norman Lear, because we fought together on so many battlefields, was not uncomfortable with putting most of his energy into the cultural wars. He founded his organization, People For the American Way and I thought that was fine. I fully support People For the American Way, but they are not so sympathetic with my arguments for economic justice. Norman and I never fought, but we had a conversation where he made it clear he was all for creating a bigger pie for everyone, but he wasn't so interested in sharing his piece of the pie or making it smaller.

"But Norman," I said, "the pie's not growing so fast anymore, and the biggest pieces keep getting bigger, while the small pieces get smaller."

"I know, Stanley, but I'm just not so comfortable with this talk about spreading the wealth and..."

I interrupted him. "Norman, we've all got more money than we'll ever need. We have to pay higher taxes. We have to…"

"I've heard this all before, Stanley. Maybe you're right, but that's not my fight. A lot of your other friends feel the same way. You're sounding more like a socialist all the time."

"What's wrong with that," I asked him.

"Nothing," he said. "But most of us are not socialists."

I guess my final break with Democratic presidential politics came after Bill Clinton's last term. For years before he was elected president, Betty and I used to have occasional dinners with Bill and Hillary at the house of our mutual friends Derek Shearer and his wife Ruth Yanatta Goldway at the Shearers' house in Santa Monica. So we knew each other fairly well. We twice even had Bill and Hillary as guests at our house in Brentwood before Bill was elected president.

I remember Bill Clinton and I had lunch in Los Angeles not long after Mayor Bradley appointed me to the police commission, and we chatted about, of all things, policing. He referred back to his days as Governor of Arkansas when he was the head of the state police. We talked about other things, but we never talked about whether he would run for president until we walked back to his hotel. We shook hands at the door. Finally, I said, "So, are you going to run or not?"

"Against George Bush?" Clinton smiled. "He just won the Gulf War. Who'd want to run against that kind of military victory?"

I shrugged. "The economy's in bad shape and he let Saddam Hussein live. Trust me, he's vulnerable."

Three months later, Bill declared his candidacy.

Betty and I have been guests of the Clintons at the White House. President Clinton gave me a great deal of totally unofficial leeway when I was pursuing Middle East peace, and I tried to be helpful for him with the Palestinians to the degree I could be. I still like the guy. If you've ever met him, you can't help liking the guy. He's so damn charming. And incredibly bright. At the beginning of his first term, I had such high hopes that he would return the Democrats to promoting the interests of the majority, who are not rich.

But Bill Clinton actually brought the Democratic Party back to power by compromising with the interests of Wall Street and the banks and the corporations. He was a significant player behind financial and corporate deregulation, and he promoted policies that have increased economic disparity in this country although, I am very sure this was not his intention. Of course he wasn't alone; most Democrats marched right alongside him. And he provided a roadmap for recent Democratic candidates including Barack Obama as well. All of this from a man who grew up in relative poverty and who I know for a fact is very sympathetic to the lower and middle classes. He really is, and he has that special connection with "the people." But economically? I have to be honest and say he bears at least some responsibility for the Great Recession of 2008 as much as it pains me to admit it.

After Clinton, I stopped being involved with presidential politics and shifted my focus to senatorial and congressional races. I do miss the action, the illusion of power, the thrill of a presidential contest, but the national body politic has become hostage to big money interests with presidential campaigns costing billions of dollars. And if someone wanted to run for the presidency, they have to raise big money through big money. The restraints imposed by federal campaign financing have been shattered by both parties, and no one but big money can compete. Besides, it's clear to me that when candidates elected through this system then attempt to govern, they have to follow policies that favor the interests that got them elected.

What's more, our economic health has become dependent on consumerism, which is in turn supported by, banks, financial corporations, Wall Street, and real estate. Since voters have all become voracious consumers, they tend to support policies, that they perceive will keep them buying. It's a vicious circle.

However, I haven't give up on electoral politics completely. In fact, Betty and I continue to do what we can with the resources we have, but we limit ourselves to those people and causes we believe can truly change the course of this tragic drift to the right.

CHAPTER FIFTEEN
This Old House

This old house once rang with laughter, this old house heard many shouts... Ain't a-gonna need this house no longer I'm a-gettin' ready to meet the saints. "This Ole House," music and lyrics by Stuart Hamblen, famously sung by Rosemary Clooney (1954) and by Bette Midler in her Rosemary Clooney tribute album of 2003.

As I finish up this story about my extraordinary life, I need to include one of the most important characters in it—not an actual person, but this house where Betty and I have lived for the past thirty years. As a good friend once remarked, I think it was Tom Hayden as he was leaving one of our many events, "This place is an institution, Stanley. After you're gone, they should just put a memorial plaque on the door and leave it just the way it is to stand forever."

The house is large but simple, modest for the neighborhood, a one-story, rambling ranch-style home overlooking Brentwood Canyon. Its most desirable feature, from our point of view, is a very good-sized open dining/living room which holds fifty to sixty people more or less comfortably; and the house's second most desirable feature is a big green grassy yard surrounded by a giant ficus, a huge California pine and various ash and elm trees. I bought Betty a lemon tree to go with another lemon tree near the edge of our garden, but it doesn't seem to be doing very well. So much for my efforts at agriculture.

Our yard is the perfect place for larger gatherings, and we have had more than 1,000 for some notable events including our annual celebration and fundraiser for the ACLU. During our most active years, Betty and I would have as many as two or sometimes even three events per week. We still host a small event at least every week, and I'm sure we will continue to do so as long as we're here and able to do so. In other words, Betty and I love this house not so much for the comfort it provides us, but for the comfort it provides those who attend the important and memorable political and charitable occasions which are held here.

We live in the Brentwood neighborhood that is famous not because Betty and I live here, but because O.J. Simpson lived just down the street. Tour buses still occasionally pass by although Simpson's house was long ago torn down and replaced by an even larger house. Actually, any house around here that does not already approach the splendor of an English country manor or a French chateau or an Italian villa is considered a tear-down. Sometimes they even tear down one mansion to build an even larger one. I'm not talking McMansions either; I'm talking *real* mansions.

Our living room, actually the entire house, has always been filled with art, some very valuable art like deKooning's "Pink Lady" which we sold to fund NPQ. There are display cases filled with Asian ceramics and a number of very unique, large colorful pieces by American craft artists like Viola Frey. Wonderful works. Betty's paintings and metal sculptures are prominently displayed. There are also sculptures by significant artists, numerous Henry Moores among them.

While both Betty and I have chosen and organized many of the events, fundraisers and book parties, I have to give credit to Betty for the insight and desire to buy this house and use it as the center for our efforts to promote the causes we believe in. And I must credit the Krims as well because they provided me with some of the original inspiration. I saw what they did with their New York home, how their townhouse became a center for so many influential people from politics, the arts, and business to get together and exchange views and ideas. That's what Betty and I had in mind when we went house hunting after we decided to live permanently in Los Angeles.

Events at our house have always been modeled more along the lines of a "salon" rather than entertainment. Typically, I will give some sort of introduction, a speaker or speakers will make short remarks on behalf of their cause, and then the room is thrown open to questions and discussion from invited guests, who are usually political activists from Hollywood, academia or the Los Angeles business community. Some in attendance have the ability to make very generous donations; some do not. Our guest list includes the rich and famous, but it is not limited to them. Betty and I decided we would use our home to promote causes we truly believe in, and therefore most of our gatherings are on behalf of liberal, leftist, progressive causes, and those who attend are mostly all progressives, lefties old and new—the famous "Westside liberals." And I have a reputation as being one of the most influential Westside liberals in Los Angeles.

But there have been those rare occasions when we've been mislead about an event we've held. There was one memorable evening when an author, an ex-CIA officer who shall remain unnamed (not Valerie Plame) had written a book "exposing" the CIA. A few moments into her talk, her remarks clearly indicated she was criticizing the intelligence community more from a right wing perspective than a liberal one. I could see the perplexed looks on the faces of many who attended. I remember Marilyn Bergman, who along with her husband Alan form one of the most respected songwriting teams in American music, grimacing, fidgeting, then actually waving her hand to get my attention. When she started firing questions at the ex-agent, they were not gentle, not kind. Then others joined in. It got fairly hostile. Afterwards Marilyn came up to me: "Stanley, what was that all about?"

"She wrote a book criticizing the CIA, Marilyn."

"Yeah, but because they weren't evil enough, Stanley."

I smiled and teased her. "She was kind of interesting though, don't you think?"

Marilyn shook her head vigorously. "No, not at all, and I'm certainly not going to buy her book." I would have to say that was pretty much the attitude of everyone there although I still think the occasion was sort of informational in a perverse, unintended way.

We've had so many politicians from all over the country, including those forums with Bill Clinton when he was still governor of Arkansas and contemplating a run for the presidency.

Betty was less excited about him than I was. When I asked her why she said, "Because he's one of those new Democrat, and he just needs the liberal vote to get the nomination, Stanley."

"I liked the guy when we met him at the Shearers," I said.

"They call him Slick Willy back in Arkansas, but his wife Hillary seems to have her head on straight."

"Well, let's have him meet people here and see what the others have to say."

It turned out to be a good evening. Clinton was, as usual, intelligent, knowledgeable and a real presence in the room. He knew how to be persuasive, to look a person in the eye and get that person to like him.

So, we supported him early on, and for awhile we were good friends. Then Clinton, like Carter, did end up governing slightly too the right of center for our tastes. However, Carter has become a better friend since he left the presidency, and in my opinion, a more interesting man, a better man, more progressive, more courageous, more outspoken. Bill Clinton seems to have also returned to his populist roots. Would that they could govern with the same attitudes.

Once I stopped being involved in presidential politics, two of my most favorite politicians and two men who are always welcome to hold fundraisers in our home are two of the more under appreciated politicians in America: Dennis Kucinich and Bernie Sanders. Dennis is a really, really bright guy, and unlike a lot of liberals, he has refused to dump his liberal ideals in the face of the rightward tilt in this country. He remains a very outspoken voice on behalf of working men and women and the true middle class. I wish he were taken more seriously on the national stage, but I fear his ideas and ideals, like mine, are out of sync with the times. That says more about the times than it does about Dennis or me.

Bernie Sanders is a national treasure. Really he is. What a wonderful, unique, straight-talking man. Although he sits with the Democratic caucus, he's the only nominal socialist to hold major office in my memory, and I believe the only self-described democratic socialist to be elected to the Senate in US history. Talk about speaking truth to power, that's Bernie Sanders. He was born in Brooklyn and lived for awhile on a kibbutz in Israel, and that's probably where he developed his basic socialist principles. Bernie has consistently fought to maintain as much national social and economic equality as possible, and he can be a thorn in the side of Democrats even as he bitterly attacks the callousness of fiscally conservative Republicans. Vermont should be praised for sending him to the Senate.

I once asked Bernie how he has been able, as a socialist, to get elected mayor of Burlington, then to the House, then to the US Senate, in a state that had traditionally been known as a bastion of bedrock Republicanism. "You know, Stanley, those New England Republicans often have values that upheld a sense of community responsibility and a commitment to fairness."

"Well, yes," I said, "but I would still think they would have great trouble voting for a man who called himself a socialist. Whatever people might think about Los Angeles, I couldn't get elected dog catcher if I described myself as a socialist."

"I'm not sure *you* could get elected to anything, Stanley," Bernie said with a wry smile.

I laughed. "Probably not," I agreed.

"Seriously, though, Stanley, I think there are people all over this country who would vote for and support democratic socialism if they were given a chance, if there were only candidates willing to honestly debate their ideas without fear of name calling. Instead they always say, 'well, I'm no socialist...' What's that crap?" I had to laugh. That's straight-talking Bernie, and I think he may be right. He reminds me of my oldest friend, my socialist friend from long ago, Al Rubin. You know, as much as I've worked hard to be a man of stature and influence, and as many times as I've met with presidents, kings, and prime ministers, I'm most proud to be a friend to men like Al and Bernie. They just genuinely care about making the world a better place for everyone.

We also held a major fundraising event for Jesse Jackson back in the 1980s when he ran for president. We were enthusiastic supporters of Jesse's candidacy and we went all out for him. It was actually also one of the few times when we've had a major snafu, although it had nothing to do with Jesse. We had arranged a beautiful 100-person sit-down dinner outside at night on the lawn, and because the dinner was outside, it was the first time we had numerous temporary ovens and lights and electronic equipment operating simultaneously. Things were going really, really well, the attendees were in a great mood, I'm sitting talking to Jesse when Bam! the power goes out. I mean all the power. It was completely dark. No one could see anything or anybody.

I heard Jesse's voice near me, "Stanley? Stanley? What the hell's going on here...Stanley?"

I didn't know what to say because I didn't know what was going on.

"Stanley?" I hear an edge of panic in Jesse's voice. He's not the only one. There are Secret Service agents trying to surround us, but they can't really see us. The other guests are fumbling about. Nervous laughter ripples through the crowd. Jesse just keeps saying, "Stanley?" Finally I attempt to reassure him everything is okay, and then, just as I'm trying to get up and investigate the problem without stumbling over something or somebody, the power came back on. We have never had that happen before or since, and I always tell Jesse we'd planned the evening that way to add a little drama. But Jesse knows I'm lying. After all, he's very aware that he provides plenty of drama all by himself.

We have also had prominent men and women from the international stage meet at the house, and probably the most wonderful, star-studded night was also the most surreal. During the Middle East negotiations, I had become friends with King Hussein of Jordan and Queen Noor, so I had invited them to our home along with, oh, if I remember correctly Warren Beatty and Annette Bening, Harrison Ford, Sela Ward and Gregory Peck. There were many others. I think Barbra Streisand was there that night as well.

Anyway, events at our house are never publicized beforehand. They are always, by Los Angeles standards anyway, private intimate evenings which is why a lot of people who might otherwise not show up are willing to attend. This was especially true for the king and queen's visit, and both Jordanian security and the US Secret Service had gone over the house and grounds with a fine-toothed comb and explosive-sniffing dogs. They had also given instructions that we had to inform the neighbors there would be no on-street parking for that evening. In other words, the visit was supposed to be very hush-hush.

However, this was also during the time when O.J. was on trial for Nicole's murder, and the neighborhood was filled with tour buses, paparazzi, bystanders, gawkers of all sorts, all hoping to get a peek at O.J. So, when expensive autos started arriving at our house and glamorous celebrities passed through our gate, people hanging out on the street near O.J.'s house gradually became aware something was going on at our place. As the word spread, bystanders started trickling toward our valet parking area. Then suddenly these huge black SUVs accompanied by police cruisers with lights flashing and sirens wailing came roaring up the street, and the trickle became a tidal wave of spectators joined by the paparazzi heading our way. By the time the king and his beautiful queen exited their vehicle, it was near chaos at the gate, but it was all very humorous because everyone seemed absolutely certain that these were very, very important people, but no one knew for certain who they were. Oh well, that's Los Angeles. I'm sure many in the crowd were convinced they'd seen some international movie star rather than the king and queen of Jordan, but a that point, the visit was hardly a secret.

As the years have passed, Betty and I have made numerous attempts to bring in a somewhat younger crowd in order to keep the tradition alive. One of the most successful attempts was when we worked with a group of younger celebrities who called themselves Young Artists United and adopted the slogan "It's cool to care." The group included Sarah Jessica Parker, Robert Downey Jr., and Alexandra Paul, along with many of their friends and fellow actors. Betty and I really loved having these young people around. They had an energy and enthusiasm that made us all feel younger and more hopeful that the future might be different.

We have always wanted to pass the tradition on to a new generation because we believe that what has been happening at our house is an important component of an involved community committed to being informed and participating in our fragile democracy. I use the term "fragile" intentionally because I believe that we have moved from an attitude that people who are privileged to have money and fame should be involved with their fellow citizens and work to make our country a better place, to an attitude by the privileged and famous who act as if they want to be separated from their community, to be private, individual, and at best, give money rather than getting involved. Personally, I believe that social media has only made this situation worse. Of course, more people are in contact with each other, but they are simultaneously, paradoxically, less involved.

Now, I'm afraid that the salon-type events that Betty and I hosted are becoming a thing of the past. I don't know, maybe they really were a product of the '60s when the politics we cared about seemed to start in people's living rooms over cookies, or at church gatherings or town meetings, at teach-ins on university campuses. People loved to talk to each other, to argue, to debate, to listen to opinions from men and women who had spent some time trying to understand and analyze where our society was headed and what we should and could do about it. I really shudder to think that the only remotely equivalent activity is now taking place on the right in the Tea Party wing of the Republican Party or out on the street with the different "Occupy" groups. I love the "occupiers" but I don't see how they are going to sway the electorate.

I know times change, and sometimes I must sound like a grouchy old man. Well, sometimes I am a grouchy old man. But if I am grouchy, it's because it seems so obvious to me that a functional democracy needs involved citizens and that these citizens need to care about each other rather than tear each other down. Even when I had some of my most bitter fights with extremely conservative members of the University of California Board of Regents or the Los Angeles Police Commission, I always found time to listen, to try and understand, to even forge friendships with my opponents that have lasted a lifetime. I don't know if that could happen now. It seems harder and harder to bring people together. I'm not certain that even if

I was thirty years younger, a spry young guy in my sixties, that I could do the job I seem to have been born to do. People have become so rigid.

And of course I know, in reality, this house will never have a plaque on the door and remain the way it is forever. As I mentioned earlier, Betty and I are already being hemmed in on all sides by the new ethos of bigger, more ostentatious, more outlandish pretentiousness. We can hardly just sit together quietly on the front lawn anymore, an old loving couple enjoying the sunshine, the trees and the cool breezes blowing in from the Pacific, the peace and quiet.

There is no peace and quiet. The house to our left has been torn down and they are building, an entire compound that will include a main house and a number of smaller houses, a tennis court, Olympic pool, running track, some sort of Republican wet dream. Our narrow street is lined each day with pick-up trucks, dump trucks, plumber's trucks, food trucks, and then there's the racket from construction equipment, jackhammers, bulldozers, cranes. If this weren't bad enough, the house to the right of us is also being smashed apart and some new monstrosity is being erected. I've grown a little hard of hearing, but even I can't believe the volume of sound arising from these construction sites. And the dirt. And the dust. And the chaos.

And, sadly, I suppose I'm getting a preview of what will happen to our house. The sculptures will be gone. The large, gentle slopping yard where so many memorable events were attended by so many national and world leaders will be ripped out. The rapacious new owners will tear the house itself down. Sure, there are those who will, for awhile, keep alive their memories of all that has happened here. Then those memories will fade as well. The property will be the site of another nondescript Mediterranean mansion, a tribute to someone's need to show off his money. It's difficult to contemplate, of course, but I know that's what will happen. It's California. Hell, it's America, the new America, not a land of opportunity, but a massive monument to greed. And that's why I am, sometimes, a grouchy old man.

EPILOGUE
Don't Get Around Much Anymore

I guess my mind's more at ease...why stir up memories? "Don't Get Around Much Anymore," lyrics by Bob Russell and music by Duke Ellington, 1940.

Well, that was my life. Of course, you don't know I'm not living that life anymore because I don't want you to know that my life out there, where you are, is pretty much over. I keep quiet. I don't say a great deal, but I make clever remarks from time to time, just enough to let you think I'm involved, but I'm actually only involved in what's going on inside, in here where the action is, and you're not in here. You're out there while I play with my riffs in my dream-state movies.

Sing, sing, sing, everybody start to sing like dee dee dee, bah bah bah dah. Now you're singin with a swing...

Last night, I finally convinced President Barack Obama to get up off his butt and start fighting—to try being a little more like Roosevelt, a true leader, a courageous battler who stood up to the rich and powerful on behalf of the common man and stop acting like Kennedy—like a handsome, articulate, intelligent manikin with a beautiful, bright involved wife and two gorgeous, active, charming children, a man who fulfills many of our dreams but doesn't really get a whole lot done. On the other hand, who am I to be discussing reality? That's what Obama said to me: "Ha, who are you to be discussing reality, Sheinbaum? You're not even really talking to me." That was unfair. He knows I can't fight back against that argument.

... everybody start to sing like dee dee dee, bah bah bah dah. Now you're singin with a swing...

But I hung in there. "Obama, you did have the most amazing opportunity," I reminded him. "You had the big chance, the main dance, center stage, ruled the White House and Congress too…nobody could have stopped you from truly pointing this country in a direction that's actually new."

…*dee dee dee, bah bah bah dah*…

"We were ready for a change, ready for that promised hope, but you had to go and be such a dope? What were you thinking? …What? What? You're the president? I can't talk to you like that? You're insulted?"

And Obama said, "Are you that out of touch, Sheinbaum? You want me to soak the rich? Really help the poor? Wake up, old, old man! Do you truly think I could have pushed a 'Sheinbaum agenda' through Congress?"

I answered, "Yes I do, sir. At least when you started, before you got scared. But you only listened to the bankers and the Wall Street crowd, and compromised with the worst of the GOP instead of listening to folks like me."

…*dee dee dee, bah bah bah dah*…

"You're nuts, Sheinbaum, this is 2011. The banks own us. So do the Chinese. We're hostage to the multinationals. Washington doesn't govern the country; people with money do. We're just paid referees trying to monitor the rules of the game."

"Okay, if that's what you choose to be. Go ahead and ignore me, Barack, but the people are restless. They want single-payer health care and they want to see the banks punished. They want to see the fat cats thinned, they want to end these costly wars, they want jobs and dignity, they want their homes, they want us all to be more equal—one big American family. They want a life and they want someone to show them how to do all of this, to tell them they *can* have these things… they want a life worth livin', don't ya' get it…"

"I get it, Sheinbaum, but I can't deliver all that."

"Yes you can! Yes you can! That was your slogan. Don't make us drink tea."

"Okay, Sheinbaum, I'll try it your way."

"If it's not too late."

"Oh, thanks, just what I wanted to hear. So, if I'm not re-elected I'll know who to blame?"

"If you lose, so what? At least you'll have tried. And you'll always know you escaped with your pride. Remember that line my goy friends all quote: *What shall profit a man if he shall gain the whole world and lose his own soul?* Don't lose your soul, Barack Obama, for the chance at another term. The people deserve better, sir, for their worn and weary pain."

…dee dee dee, bah bah bah dah. Now you're singin with a swing…

Well, now you see how much fun it is to live my fantasy life. I just convinced Obama to put up a fight! I love it! I'm still involved. Now I've got to consider what else I can do. Keep pushing, keep pushing. It keeps me alive. I have to keep pushing or the outside will die. And I'm not ready to die, not yet…okay, in truth, some days I am, but I'm not quite ready to go just yet…not ready…not quite…Gotta' talk to Netanyahu, to Julian Assange, to Warren Buffet, to…to…Jean Harlow…

I don't want to quit on the world like poor little Jean! She left the world when I was fifteen…and she was only 26…

…I've flown around the world in a plane. I've settled revolutions in Spain. The North Pole I have charted, but I can't get started with you…

Jean, Jean? I have a cardboard cutout of you in my office. I do. Someone had it made for my 91st birthday, and I look at you every time I pass by. You renew latent lust, and I must say it's a kick to pick up where we left off 76 years ago…Oh my…

…You're so supreme, lyrics I write of you, scheme just for a sight of you, dream, both day and night of you. And what good does it do?

She's gone. I guess it's better that way. So…what are we doing? What's going on? What are we achieving? I just don't get it. We could *do* so much more. We could *be* so much better. Let's get going. Going, going, gone…Where has all the money gone? To the bankers? To the rich? Not to the poor, that's for sure. Not to the middle class. No, no, no. Warren Buffet's got it right. Let's spread the wealth around. Why not? What's wrong? What's really going on?

Uh, oh, here's the president again. Good talker. Very good talker… excellent speeches…talk, talk, talk…"Barack, Barack, why do you keep coming back?"

"You're ruining my presidency, Sheinbaum. I propose new programs, they won't listen to me. No spending they say, they rejected my plan."

"Barack, Barack Obama, time to put on a show. We need the flim-flam, the hoochie-coochie so the people will know you're their man, you're for them, they need to see that you care. Convince them of that and they'll follow you anywhere."

…Oh 't ain't what you do, it's the way that you do it. 'T ain't what you do, it's the way that you do it…That's what gets results…

"Go on, Obama, stop getting gray hair. You're stressed and alone because you've strayed so far from home—from what made you believe, from what made you care. Hey Obama, what's wrong with a little class warfare? The rich do it. They screw the poor and the middle-classes too. They just hide their maneuvers so people can't see the money. It doesn't trickle down like rivers toward the sea…more like oil from a pipette, drip…drop…drip…"

'T ain't what you do, it's the way that you do it. That's what gets results…

"Results, results…that's what my mother was always pounding into me. Results. Hated it. Hated her. For a long time I didn't listen, but when I got started, after I married Betty, I seldom if ever second-guessed myself, and the more I forged ahead, then the more courageous I became. Hey, for awhile there, I was the most hated Jew in America…by other Jews anyway. Sure, I want to be loved, respected, admired. Don't we all, Barack? But I didn't waste time agonizing. I raised the money, introduced contacts, traveled the world and brought enemies together because it was the thing to do and somebody needed to do it. Go ahead; it's fun. More fun than trying to get people to say they like you when they aren't going to like you anyway."

'T ain't what you do, it's the way that you do it.

Jews…Jewish…Israel…I need to have a word with Netanyahu, "Prime Minister Benjamin Netanyahu, sir, Bibi! Listen! It's time to get this Middle East peace thing done. The Arab Spring? Its tides of change are not washing gently against Israeli shores. What in the hell are you waiting for?"

I'm as restless as a willow in a windstorm. I'm as jumpy as a puppet on a string. I'd say that I had spring fever, but I know it isn't spring…

"That's the problem, Bibi. It isn't really spring. More like late fall. Now's the time before winter settles in, maybe a nuclear winter—one we won't forget. Are we blinded by the sandstorms of time? The horrors, yes, the horrors of what we've endured! We cannot forget. Never forget. But what is the lesson we're not to forget? Maybe it's how to recognize threat, and take action to secure our future. How? After all, we've already got the guns and the bombs to obliterate our enemies."

I am starry-eyed and vaguely discontented, like a nightingale without a song to sing. Oh, why should I have spring fever, when it isn't even spring?

"Can't we give peace a chance, Bibi?"

"No."

"Can't we give a lot more in negotiations?"

"No."

"Can't we end this whole mess where we always have to talk as enemies?"

"No."

I keep wishing I were somewhere else, walking down a strange new street...

"How long can we go on like this always saying, no?"

"Forever, if need be. Forever and then longer. Never forget!"

I guess some arguments I can't win, even in my fantasies. I have cared about Israel and peace in the Middle East more than any other issue in my lifetime. I have given more to Israel and peace in the Middle East, and still peace eludes me. I truly am just a man. Weak and fallible. But if we care too much about how things are going to turn out, then we wouldn't do anything, would we? I mean, there were no guarantees. There never are. And in the end...

And in the end...does it matter? There's no heaven; no hell. Only the memories, *thanks for the memories*...Ah, why do Bob Hope and Barack Obama keep pushing into my riffs? I want Benny Goodman, Ella Fitzgerald, the Dorseys, Billy Holiday and, and Jean Harlow.

No! No, no more fantasy as the end draws near. I do not want Jean Harlow. I want Betty. Betty...

Some things that happened for the first time seem to be happening again...

"Ah, Betty, we did so many wonderful things, met so many wonderful people, went to so many wonderful places. They were real, weren't they? They really happened?"

"Yes, Stanley."

We seemed to float right through the air. Heavenly songs seemed to come from everywhere...

"But how did we do it? I'm just an ordinary guy."

"But a man with courage, the courage to try."

"I think it was more than that, Betty. I think it was you."

And now when there's moonglow, way up in the blue, I'll always remember that moonglow gave me you...

"Why, thank you, Stanley.

"No, thank you, Betty."

If you enjoyed reading about Stanley K. Sheinbaum, we invite you to go to **stanleysheinbaum.com** for more information. While there, you might also want to purchase a copy of the excellent, critically acclaimed documentary DVD about Stanley's life, "Citizen Stan."

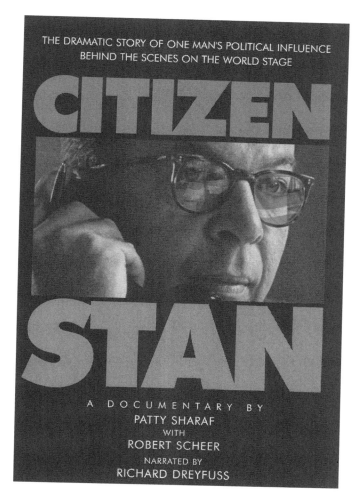

THE DRAMATIC STORY OF ONE MAN'S POLITICAL INFLUENCE
BEHIND THE SCENES ON THE WORLD STAGE

CITIZEN
STAN

A DOCUMENTARY BY
PATTY SHARAF
WITH
ROBERT SCHEER
NARRATED BY
RICHARD DREYFUSS

Stanley K. Sheinbaum

Made in the USA
Charleston, SC
31 January 2012